OUT OF THE WILDERNESS

By Susan E. Hilliard

Illustrated by Ned O.

STANDARD PUBLISHING
Cincinnati, Ohio   24-03981

Library of Congress Cataloging-in-Publication Data

Hilliard, Susan E.
   Out of the wilderness / Susan E. Hilliard.
     p. cm. —(Decide your own adventure ; 1)
   Summary: The reader makes choices about the unfolding of Moses's life.
   ISBN 0-87403-581-3
   1. Moses (Biblical leader)—Juvenile literature. 2. Bible. O.T.—Biography—Juvenile literature. 3. Plot-your-own stories. [1. Moses (Biblical leader) 2. Bible stories—O.T. 3. Plot-your-own stories.] I. Title. II. Series: Hilliard, Susan E. Decide your own adventure ; 1.
BS580.M6H55 1989
222'.1092—dc20
[B]
                                                89-4492
                                                     CIP
                                                       AC

Edited by Theresa C. Hayes

Copyright ©1989 by the
STANDARD PUBLISHING Company, Cincinnati, Ohio.
A Division of STANDEX INTERNATIONAL Corporation.
Printed in U.S.A.

Attention, Reader!

You cannot read this book as you would any other. You are embarking upon a very special quest for truth. The object of this particular journey—your quest—will be revealed to you before you begin your journey through time, in a chariot of fire.

During your quest, you will sometimes be allowed to direct your own adventure by choosing between alternative events, or times, in history. When you make your choice, the chariot will take you swiftly to the time and location you have indicated.

When you find the chariot, be sure to look for two parchment scrolls in it. The largest scroll is a vital archive (recorded facts) regarding your quest, and can aid you in making the right choices. A smaller parchment contains the quest—the object of your journey. Also in the chariot, you will find rules for your travel, and appropriate clothing.

And now, begin the adventure!

The Chariot

A chariot of fire stands before you. The chariot itself seems solid enough, although it appears to be completely in flames. Your heart pounding with excitement, you step closer and notice that the fire is not hot—only pleasantly warm. Through the shimmering flames you see a beautiful horse, hitched to the chariot, standing patiently. The animal seems so calm that you find your heart is not thumping quite so violently, and you hesitantly step onto the chariot. Nothing happens. You are surrounded by flames, yet nothing is burning. You step farther into the chariot, and notice a plain wooden box on the floor. Upon the box is written "Rules for Travel." You open the box.

On the inside of the lid, you read...

Rules for Travel

You must follow these rules on your journey. If you do not, the chariot will return you to the present and you will never be able to complete your quest.

I. You may not change history in any way—you are only an observer.
II. You may choose only from the alternatives that you are given.
III. You may not bring twentieth-century customs, clothing, or equipment with you. During your journey, you may tell no one where or what time you are from.
IV. You may not bring any souvenirs of your journey home with you.

You will find that language differences will not be a problem for you—you will automatically think and speak in the language of your host place and time.

Inside the box is something made from green cloth. You pull it out, and see that beneath the cloth, in the bottom of the box, is a rough sketch of what appears to be an Egyptian man in a skirt. Oh no! You glance again at the green cloth—it's a skirt, alright! Well, you might as well get dressed for your travels. You change quickly into the skirt—which itches—and toss your clothes and shoes out of the chariot into a nearby bush. The horse seems impatient now, and begins pawing the ground. In growing excitement, you drop to your knees in the small chariot, searching for the parchment. Your hands grope in the dark forward corners; it is difficult to see. At last—your hands touch two things that feel like cylinders of paper. Eagerly, you draw them out. Anxious to discover the purpose of your journey, you unroll the smaller scroll and read...

The Quest

You are instructed to go to the time of Moses, and to find out why Moses was not allowed by God to actually enter the promised land.

Moses was called to deliver the people of Israel from bondage in Egypt. But why were they slaves in Egypt in the first place? How did they escape? Where did they go after they escaped? Most importantly, though, your quest is to determine why Moses, who led the children of Israel out of captivity and to the very borders of the promised land, was not permitted to enter it. Be careful—these were dangerous times!

You hurriedly unroll the second, larger scroll, reading through it quickly. On this second scroll, you find written...

Archives

I. In approximately 1580 B.C., the Egyptians overthrew their foreign rulers, the Hyksos. At this time, the Egyptians destroyed the Hyksos capital at Avaris, near Goshen. Egypt was reunited under a native Egyptian pharaoh who ruled from Thebes.

II. For the numerous construction projects under Rameses II, an enormous supply of bricks was necessary. So slaves, captured foreigners, and even wandering nomads, were forced to work at the endless and arduous task of brick-making.

III. To make bricks, mud from the Nile was added to sand and chopped straw; this mixture was mixed with wooden mattocks and trodden down. The mixture was then placed in wooden molds and left to dry in the sun for eight days. Sometimes the bricks were stamped with the pharaoh's own seal.

IV. Tall papyrus reeds grew by the banks in abundance. These reeds were also called bulrushes. From the papyri came rope, baskets, mats, sandals, small boats (made from bundles of reeds bound together), and even "paper" (thin slices of the soft pulp).

V. Because of a terrible famine in Palestine in about 1,650 B.C., Joseph's entire family settled in Egypt, where Joseph held the position of governor, second in command to Pharaoh. There, the population of the Israelites grew enormously over the next two to four-hundred years.

VI. "Moses" was an Egyptian name—it sounded like the Hebrew word for "draw out." The pharaoh's daughter knew that the baby in the Nile was Hebrew, and her name for him was a play on words.

VII. Pharaoh's daughter sent Moses to live with his own mother until he was three. At that time she brought him to Pharaoh's palace to be raised as her own son.

VIII. In the plagues that the Lord sent upon Egypt, He executed judgement upon the "gods" of Egypt, clearly demonstrating His power to all the people.

IX. Because of their unbelief, not one Israelite twenty years of age or older (except Joshua and Caleb), who had seen the Lord's miracles in Egypt and the Sinai, set foot in the promised land.

X. The children of Israel wandered in the wilderness for forty years. Although God sustained them daily with food and water, most of them continually complained and wanted to return to Egypt.

You decide you had better keep this scroll with you, for you have a feeling it might come in handy. You stuff it into the waist of your skirt, where the folds of cloth hide it completely.

After you've stuffed the scroll into the folds of cloth, you pick up the leather reins and hold them loosely. Now what? You pull the smooth leather taut, and suddenly...

You find yourself sitting on the ground (no chariot of fire is visible now) beside a slow-moving, muddy river. The sky above is incredibly blue, and the air is hot and still. The only sound is the muted music of the river and a light breeze moving the numerous reeds by the water's edge. You stand carefully, glad that you are none the worse for your time traveling. But where are you?

The sound of laughter makes you jump—you already feel ridiculous in this outfit. You whirl around to glare in the direction of the laughter, and see a girl—about your age—shaking with laughter and pointing at you. Humiliated, you stalk angrily toward her. Suddenly she is joined by an entire group of girls, all staring at you. You recognize that they are dressed in Egyptian clothing—plain tunics of white cloth.

"How white his skin is—look!" The girls all seem curious, and you are relieved to learn that they are not laughing at your skirt. You hear a distant shout, and the girls scurry away toward the sound of the voice.

Alone again—you've got to *do* something, or you'll never get started on your quest. The sound of voices seems to come from somewhere downstream, just beyond a bend in the river. Aware that you'd best be careful in a strange time and place, you move through the tall reeds, following the river toward the sound of voices. The ground is rising slightly, and suddenly, you find yourself

at the top of a low hill. Below you, at the water's edge, is an Egyptian man, dressed like you, with an enormous whip. The whip cracks violently over the naked back of an old man, straining to

carry two buckets affixed to a wooden yoke over his shoulders.

"Hurry up, old man! You Apiru are *all* idle good-for-nothings!" The old man shuffles faster, his face twisted with pain.

To your horror, you see that there are scores of men and boys carrying buckets, and many Egyptian overseers—all with whips. Cries, groans, and the constant, gun-like reports of whips pierce the burning air. The slaves--for so they must be—carry empty buckets to the river's edge and fill them with mud. They then raise the yoke to their shoulders and move toward a pit about twenty yards away. There they empty their buckets of mud and return to the water's edge.

Your cautious steps take you closer to the pit. Here you see more slaves, their lower legs and feet covered with mud. They appear to be treading in a mixture of sand, straw, and mud. Here, too, are still more Egyptian overseers. You see an older man fall, face down, in the mud. An angry Egyptian whips the old man viciously, but he does not move. Sickened, you want to go far away from this place of cruelty, and you retrace your steps in the direction from which you came.

After what seems like hours of cautious, rustling steps through the reeds, you sink down by the edge of the water. There is no relief from the relentless sun; you are tired, hungry, and thirsty. Desperate, you cup your hands in the muddy river and drink, then dunk your head with relief in the cool water. The sound of approaching voices makes you retreat into the reeds in a hurry.

From your hiding place you see a woman carrying a baby, a little boy, and a girl approaching the water. These people do not look at all like Egyptians—their clothing is completely different. The little boy darts suddenly out of sight, and the woman kneels quietly at the river bank. Even from here, you can see that the woman looks sad, as she kisses her baby and lowers it into a basket that the girl has placed on the ground.

This *must* be Moses, you think excitedly, and

you start forward. "OW!" Sharp little fingernails bite deeply into your legs, your knees are suddenly pinned together, and you fall flat on your face. You catch a glimpse of a stormy face, as the little boy's plump fists flail furiously at you.

"Hey, wait!" you manage to shout, "I'm not going to hurt anybody!" The child's blows slow a bit, and you raise yourself up on an elbow to face him. "If that's your family over there, they have nothing to fear from me!"

You guess that this little boy is only about three years old. His face is flushed with fury, and his chest is heaving. "Who are you?" he asks gruffly, with only a very small quaver betraying his little boy's fear.

You sit up slowly, watching a tear trace a path through the dust on the flushed little face. "You don't need to worry about me," you say earnestly. "Is your mother putting Moses in the river so the pharaoh's men won't drown him?"

A grubby fist wipes the tear away impatiently. "His name isn't Moses!" he answers roughly. "But that *is* the reason she is putting him in that basket. The pharaoh's daughter is just downstream, and my mother is hoping that she'll see my baby brother and rescue him. We can't hide him anymore—it's too dangerous."

A ragged sigh escapes the child as he looks back at his mother. "I've got to get back," he says sadly, squaring his shoulders bravely. "I'm sorry I hit you, but I was afraid you were going to tell the Egyptians what we are doing!"

"Aaron!" the woman's voice calls softly. "Come quickly!" The little boy darts away, his hand waving a brief farewell.

Your eyes are drawn to the closed basket, floating gently downstream. The child said that the baby's name isn't Moses, but should you follow it anyway? Undecided, you look back to where the mother was standing, but she has completely vanished, as has the girl.

You jump as a firm hand descends forcefully upon your shoulder, and a deep voice growls "So you decided you had no need of school today, eh?" A tall Egyptian man, whose twinkling eyes tell you he is not as gruff as his voice, has you in a very firm grip. "Well, boy, what should I do with you then?"

You take a deep breath, for you know that the basket is floating farther and farther away. Should you try to run away from the Egyptian in order to follow the baby? Or should you trust this man, whose face is kind and who is probably too strong for you to escape from anyway?

**If you decide
to follow the basket, go to page 21.**

**If you decide
to trust the Egyptian, go to page 50.**

(You Have Decided to Search for the Chariot)

Cautiously, you pad silently down the empty corridor, down the narrow stairs, and out the front door into the dark street. The deep shadows are eerie and disconcerting; the night air is much chillier than you had thought it would be. You begin to jog along the basalt-paved road; statues loom ominously in unexpected places.

You find yourself now on an unpaved, dusty road; you strain to hear the familiar sound of light wind through the reeds by the river's edge. You expect that if you will find the chariot at all, it will be in the same area from which you began your quest. Finally, you are past the last house on the road, your steps slowing now from fatigue. The moon has not yet risen, and the night sky is ink-black. Stars hang suspended from the velvet heavens. There are no familiar sounds, and your steps falter to a stop. You are completely alone, in a strange time and a strange place.

You stand there, frozen with the enormity of being so totally isolated from everything familiar. There is no sign of your chariot—and you have the feeling that it is not going to appear like magic, just because you want it to.

With a tired sigh, you turn your steps back in

the direction from which you have come. You realize that you will have to return to Semnet's house—if you are lucky enough to find it. You wish you had considered the possibility of having to find your way back; you would have paid much better attention to direction! You remember uncomfortably that you have read that some of the Egyptian religions practice human sacrifice—and you hope that no one is out looking for a candidate tonight!

With a sigh of enormous relief, you recognize Semnet's house just down the street. Swiftly and quietly, you let yourself in—it is lucky for you that Semnet doesn't lock his door. Just as cautiously as you left, you creep back up the stairs and into Hapu's room, where he is still sleeping soundly. You sink down on your mat thankfully, feeling relieved that you are back none the worse for wear.

Go to page 29.

(You Have Decided to Go Back in Time)

You are suddenly very unsure you have chosen wisely. The voice suggested that you go forward, and you decided to do just the opposite. How far back are you going to find yourself?

Go to page 93.

(You Have Decided to Follow the Basket)

You wheel quickly on your heels and run as fast as you can away from the Egyptian. Your training in track comes in handy, as you hear his steps becoming farther and farther behind yours. The tall reeds do not offer much resistance to your progress, but the intense heat and excitement slow you down. Your heart pounding and your throat dryly stinging, you stop for a moment, to wipe the sweat from your forehead with the back of your hand. The basket is within sight again, floating gently downriver.

You walk more cautiously now, for the river is making a wide bend, and you hear voices close by. As you round the bend of the river, you notice that the land falls gently. In the lower-lying area at the curve, you see a collection of buildings glistening white in the sun. It is from here that the voices float toward you in the shimmering heat—twenty or thirty women are wading in the shallow water at the river's edge. They are obviously Egyptians, for their hair is ebony, and their clothing looks exactly like that found in your social studies book under "Ancient Egyptian Noblewomen."

The basket rounds the bend, and is spotted by one of the women. You drop to your knees and

crawl now, for you know that you dare not be seen. Peering intently through the bulrushes, you see that all the women are looking at the basket, and you can hear the excitement in their voices as they lift the lid and find the baby inside. One woman lifts the baby gently out, and cradles it lovingly. The woman must be someone important, you think, because she is wearing far more sparkling jewelry than anyone else.

You strain to hear what she is saying, but it is difficult to hear her voice over the noise of the

crying baby and the excited chatter of the other women. To your amazement, you see the girl whom you saw with the baby's mother when the basket was first placed in the river. She speaks quietly to the woman holding the baby. The woman nods, and the girl splashes out of the river and sets off running back upriver.

You really want to know what is going on, so you creep closer. It could be that the girl is Miriam, Moses' sister, but if you could just get a *little* nearer....

A huge hand comes from nowhere and holds you like a steel vise. An equally huge face looms down at you from an impossible height.

"Away with you, boy!" he roars, and you feel yourself picked up and thrown through the air. You land several feet from this fearsome giant of a man, who is striding toward you with spear in hand, his menacing face filled with fury.

"No one spies on the pharaoh's harem while I stand guard!" he bellows. No one needs to tell you that you had better get out of here fast if you want to remain in one piece! You take to your heels, and run faster than you have ever run in your life. The guard's shouts follow you for a short distance, then stop. You allow your steps to slow, as it occurs to you that you are no longer in danger. But what are you going to do next?

You are beginning to get awfully tired and thirsty; your stomach tells you that it has been a long time since that one piece of toast and jelly you had this morning. You continue to walk slowly through the reeds at the river's edge, not paying particularly close attention to where you are going. You are thinking that Egypt is not very interesting — all hot sun and reeds — when you are abruptly startled out of your daydream.

"So *there* you are! You outran me, boy, but I had a feeling that you'd be back this way soon. Did you run into the harem's guard?"

You look up, startled, and find yourself staring into the face of the Egyptian man who had first caught you. His black eyes are twinkling, and his white teeth dazzle in his darkly-complected face. He seems infinitely preferable to the huge angry giant you've just run away from.

"Yes—only he sort of ran into me," you answer. The Egyptian shakes with laughter, and pats you on the back in a friendly manner.

"No wonder you're so pale! Now you see what kind of trouble you can get yourself into when you play truant from school, eh? So, what should I do with you?" You fall into step beside him; he seems kind, and you really don't know what else to do for the moment.

Continue on page 26.

(Going With the Egyptian)

"I'll tell you what," the Egyptian says kindly. "I'll let you decide. From the look of you, you've had quite a day. Do you want to go back to school, or would you like to go on home?" With a jolt, you realize that you don't know what to tell him. You can't go home, because your mission is not yet complete—in fact, it has hardly started. You also know that you can't tell him anything about the mission.

"Well," you stammer, "I don't really have any place to go." *At least that's the truth*, you think miserably. The Egyptian's arm tightens around your shoulder, and he smiles.

"So that's the way of it, eh? I'm thinking you have the look of a well-born boy who has run away from too many beatings at home and at school! You have nothing to fear from me, boy. I have a son about your age, and he is schooled at the temple," he says, his voice warm with pride. "Not all scribe schools are as advanced as the temple school; I was beaten myself when I was a youth, but I want none of that for my son."

Egypt is sounding worse and worse, you think worriedly. *What am I going to do?* You realize with a start that the Egyptian has stopped walking, and has asked you a question.

"So, what would you do? Let me take you to my son's school now, or call it a day and come on home with me? I'll be glad to give you a home until you've made up your mind what you need to do." The Egyptian's face is kind, but you have no idea what might be best. Should you try the school, or should you go home with him?

If you decide
to go to school, turn to page 117.

If you decide to go home with
the Egyptian, turn to page 30.

(You Have Decided to Go Back to Egypt)

You realize suddenly with startling clarity that you have probably made the wrong choice. Moses killed the Egyptian *before* he was told to lead the Hebrews out of bondage—that *couldn't* have been the reason he was prevented from entering the promised land. Fleetingly, you wish you had taken time to think before you made your decision. Next time, you resolve, you will not be so hasty.

Go to page 11.

(You Decide to Go to Sleep)

You fall into a light sleep, but sound slumber eludes you. Some time later, you are certain you hear a sound in the corridor outside your room. You look out into the hall, and see that the chariot of fire is there waiting, illuminating the entire corridor.

This time, you know that the fire will not burn you, and you do not hesitate to climb aboard. Suddenly, you realize that there is a voice speaking—seeming to come from the beautiful white steed, although the horse's mouth is not moving. The voice tells you that the chariot will be brought to you at the proper times, and that sometimes—but not always—you will be given a choice of times to travel to. "On some occasions, I may suggest a choice; but, of course, you are always free to make your own decision," the voice continues. "Now, I would like to take you a number of years into the future, into the time of Moses' young adulthood. Shall we go, or do you have a different choice?"

The voice falls silent. Should you take the suggestion or should you try to get this quest accomplished in a hurry, by asking the chariot to take you to the time that would answer the questions?

**If you take the suggestion, go to page 80.
If you want a shortcut, go to page 144.**

(You Have Decided to Go Home With the Egyptian)

You realize that you have been somewhat shaken by the abrupt transition from the familiar to the strange; you also decide that if you can avoid it, you'd really rather not try an Egyptian school—today or *any* day!

"Well, it's awfully nice of you to invite me to your home, sir. I don't think I'd do too well at school today," you answer gratefully.

"Fine with me, boy," the Egyptian says kindly. "My house is not far from here, and I was on my way home anyway when I caught you. By the way, my name is Semnet. I am a craftsman for Pharaoh, by trade," he continues proudly.

"What craft?" you inquire curiously.

Semnet explains that he has been carving since he was a boy. He is interesting to talk to, and you walk briskly along, without taking much notice of your surroundings.

At last you begin looking around you, and see that as you have been walking, you have reached the city limits. You are now walking swiftly along a dusty street, lined on both sides with houses made from sun-baked bricks, whitewashed and sparkling. Semnet stops before a two-story structure, opens the door, and ushers you inside.

You enter a spacious hall, made even more attractive by gaily-colored wall hangings. Two or three small tables hold beautifully-carved animals, polished to gleaming brightness. Semnet leads you up a narrow staircase, down a wide hall, and out onto the rooftop, which overlooks a small garden below. Someone obviously spends a great deal of time on this rooftop, for there are cushions, bowls, and many other comforts here.

The remainder of the day passes pleasantly. You meet Semnet's wife, enjoy some delicious fruits and bread, and listen to the gurgling music of the fountain in the garden below. Soon a boy about your age bounds out, and Semnet introduces his son, Hapu.

After the sun sets and dinner is finished, you and Semnet and Hapu lounge comfortably on the flat rooftop, enjoying the cool evening breezes. You are beginning to be uncomfortable about learning nothing; you realize that you'll never finish your quest this way. Semnet is fortunately very incurious about your past, so you feel safe in asking him some questions about the Apiru.

"Semnet, why did the Apiru ever come here to begin with?" you ask curiously.

"Well," he answers slowly, "I only know what few bits and pieces I've heard; I don't know how much truth there is in it." The Egyptian settles himself more comfortably on his cushions, and stares meditatively into the small fire he has built.

"I have heard that many, many generations

ago, a Hebrew named Joseph was brought here as a slave. There was some treachery involved in his family, but I don't know anything about that. He was a good man, and very intelligent; he worked diligently, but for some reason he was thrown in jail. Here is where the story really gets interesting," says Semnet, obviously warming to the tale.

"While he was in prison," he continues, "two of the other prisoners had dreams that really bothered them. When Joseph heard that they were truly upset, he asked them to tell him their dreams to see if he could interpret them. After he had heard them, he predicted that one prisoner—the butler—would be freed, and that the other—the baker—would be hanged.

"Well, just what Joseph had predicted came true. The butler was freed, and the baker hanged. Some time later, the pharaoh's magicians could not explain the meaning of his dreams, and that is when the butler remembered Joseph. To get to the end of the tale," says Semnet, "Joseph was brought before the pharaoh to interpret the dreams. That pharaoh was so impressed, he made Joseph the governor of all Egypt."

Semnet takes a long, thirsty drink from his cup and continues. "So, the former slave became Pharaoh's trusted governor over all the viziers of the land, and thus very powerful. I'm not sure of the details after that, but there seems to have been a famine in Joseph's own country. His family traveled to Egypt to buy grain from the pharaoh, and the family was reunited and eventually moved to Egypt. The Hebrews prospered, for our pharaohs at that time were Hyksos—foreigners themselves. The Egyptian people overthrew the Hyksos, but from that time until now, the Hebrews' lot has declined; now you see them as slaves."

Now you understand how the children of Israel have come to be slaves in Egypt. You'd like to learn a few more details, but Semnet has told you all he knows. Your eyelids have begun to droop a bit, and you are happy when you and Hapu are sent to bed.

Hapu leads you into a small room, where two

thick mats are ready on the floor. You throw yourself down onto the mat gratefully. Almost before you pull the rough blanket over yourself, you realize that you are falling asleep. It has been quite a day.

Hours later, you wake with moonlight streaming into the window. You hear Hapu's quiet breathing on the other mat, and you get up carefully. You feel refreshed, and ready to get on with your quest. You look out of the window at the sleeping city, hoping to see the chariot of fire—but you see nothing. Should you go outside and search for it, or should you just go back to sleep and figure it out in the morning?

If you decide
to go back to sleep, turn to page 29.

If you decide
to search for the chariot, go to page 18.

Decide Your Own Adventure **35**

(You Have Decided to Follow Moses)

You thread your way through the quiet, mourning crowd. Most are sobbing openly at the loss of Moses. At the outer edge of the crowd, you break into a run; you can see the solitary figure of Moses making his way toward Mount Nebo just west of the encampment.

You run swiftly, and arrive at the foot of Mount Nebo, where you stop, panting. Moses has just begun his ascent of the mountain.

Go to page 100.

(You Have Decided to Go to Midian)

Before you know it, you find yourself sitting in a clump of scratchy bushes; you are terribly hot, and thoroughly uncomfortable. You look around you, and see that you are in an oasis, surrounded by desert as far as you can see. The sun above beats down fiercely, and you are glad of the shade of the huge palm trees clustered around you.

The sound of bleating sheep makes you turn in the direction of the noise; you see several young women walking across the scorching desert floor, leading a flock toward the oasis. From your uncomfortable seat, you can see the entire oasis, which is larger than you expected it to be. Your bushes are on a hill, and as you look down through the palm trees, you can see Moses stretched out flat—his right arm shielding his eyes as if in sleep.

On the other side of the oasis, in the direction opposite from that of the approaching women, a group of what appear to be shepherds—or so you guess from their crooked staffs and scraggly goats—are also approaching. They all must be coming here for water, you decide, for you see a large well in what is roughly the center of the oasis.

The young women reach the well first, and begin filling skin bags with water. They then take the water over to a rough trough among the palm trees, and pour it into the trough for the sheep to drink. Suddenly you hear shouts, and you see that the shepherds have arrived, and are frightening the young women away from the well. *Hey, that's not fair; the girls were first!* you think to yourself. The shepherds are bullies, just like you've seen plenty of times yourself!

As you watch, a furious Moses bursts into sight. You can see from here that he is older than

38 Decide Your Own Adventure

you thought; he is not a young man—he must be your parents' age! With an angry roar and fists flying, Moses quickly drives the shepherds away. The seven young women are huddled anxiously in the distance, wondering what to do about this new threat—for the sheep must be watered.

Moses calmly picks up one of the skin bags which, in her haste to get away from the bullies, one of the women has dropped. He fills it with water, then crosses to pour it into the trough. The women approach him hesitantly; you can see that they quickly become more comfortable, and soon they are all talking together while the thirsty sheep are being watered.

You wonder if you will be accepted as readily as you were in Egypt, with practically no questions asked about where you have come from. Deciding to risk it, you quietly approach the group. No one seems at all surprised at your presence; the young women are pleasant, and treat you like a member of the family. The sheep finish drinking, and the girls go home—only to return immediately to invite Moses to come home with them, for their father has said he would like to thank Moses for helping his daughters. You tag along at the rear of the flock, trying to look like you really know how to herd sheep.

After walking for what feels like hours, you see tents in the distance, and you hope that soon you'll be able to sit down. You decide to just keep to the back, and listen.

An older man, dressed in a tunic and a heavy, striped outer garment stands in front of the largest tent, watching your approach. His head is covered with a turban, and his beard is long and white. As Moses nears the tent, the older man is the first to speak. "Peace be on you," he says formally.

"And on you, peace," answers Moses with courtesy.

The older man places his right hand on Moses' left shoulder and kisses his right cheek; then places his left hand on Moses' right shoulder, kissing his left cheek. He introduces himself as Jethro, the father of the girls. Moses is ushered ceremoniously into the tent, where you follow quietly.

The tent is larger than the others, you notice, and there is a spear standing by the entrance. The fabric of the tent is coarse, but the interior is surprisingly cool. Rugs cover the ground, and a coarse curtain appears to divide the tent into at least one other room beyond. In the center of this area, a fire burns brightly, surrounded by stones. You see a large pot resting on the stones, and notice that a delicious smell fills the tent. You discover that you are ravenously hungry.

As soon as Moses enters the tent, he removes his sandals; you quickly do the same. You watch in interest as a servant hurries forward with a basin of water and a towel, and washes Moses' feet. As the servant dries Moses' feet, another respectfully rubs a lightly-scented oil into his hair. You are apparently accepted here, as Jethro smiles kindly at you, and bids you be seated. Other boys your age begin to crowd into the tent behind their fathers, all carefully removing their shoes before entering. *A guest is really a big deal here*, you think; everyone seems to be interested in this strange visiting Egyptian.

After everyone's hands have been washed in

much the same manner as Moses' feet were washed, the men and boys all sit cross-legged on the brightly-colored mats covering the ground. There are no women or girls in evidence now. You are astonished at the meal that follows—the huge pot you saw on the stones by the fire is placed in the center of everyone, along with a basket containing many small, flat loaves of bread. You all help yourself to a loaf, and dip it into the mixture in the pot. It is delicious! There is fruit, and light fig cakes. You eat until you are stuffed; everyone seems to accept you as part of the family.

You spend several days and nights here—the people are friendly and kind, and you are learning a lot about life in the desert. You help tend the sheep, and listen around the fire at night to the men's stories of their lives. You can understand how this simple life would be very difficult to leave; although the desert is harsh, and life sometimes hard, the people work together and are very close.

You awake early one morning to watch the sun rise—the air has that special pre-dawn stillness. To your disappointment, you see the chariot waiting for you a little way from the tent. You

Decide Your Own Adventure 43

climb reluctantly into the vehicle, as you think regretfully that your time here is finished. You hear the now-familiar voice telling you that you must skip forward in time.

"You may choose between three alternatives," the voice says. "You may return to Egypt, you may go forward forty years to see Moses preparing to return to Egypt, or you may see with your own eyes what Moses sees on the mountain in Midian."

Thoughts swirl and jostle each other; what is the correct choice? You're not sure that you want to see Moses age forty years in a split second. You wonder if Moses will not be allowed to enter the promised land because he killed the Egyptian—returning to Egypt might answer that question. Or, perhaps the answer will be revealed by whatever Moses will see on the mountain in Midian. You take the reins in your hand and make your decision.

If you decide to return to Egypt, turn to page 28.

If you decide to go forward 40 years in Midian, turn to page 107.

If you decide to see what Moses sees, turn to page 55.

(You Have Decided to See the Giving of the Law)

You find yourself at the edge of the Hebrew encampment; hundreds of thousands of tents fill the valleys between the huge, craggy, granite mountains surrounding you. You wander into the camp, and notice that many people seem to be hurrying somewhere. The crowd of people grows, and you follow closely.

You follow them to the foot of a rugged mountain, where you see smoke rising black against the sky. Peering through the throng, you see that the smoke comes from an altar; beyond the altar is a statue of a bull, gleaming golden in the glow of the fire. Before the altar, you see people dancing and singing drunkenly. As you watch, more and more join in. Soon they all seem to be in a frenzy of dancing. *Where is Moses, or Aaron*, you wonder in alarm. Your scalp prickles, and you know that you don't want to stay here any longer. Disgusted and upset, you turn to make your way out of the excited crowd.

"What's the matter? Don't you like the beautiful bull god that Aaron made for us?" sneers a young woman standing next to you. "We're going to need *some* kind of god, stuck in the desert like we are!"

"Where is Moses?" you ask, trying not to sound as disapproving as you feel.

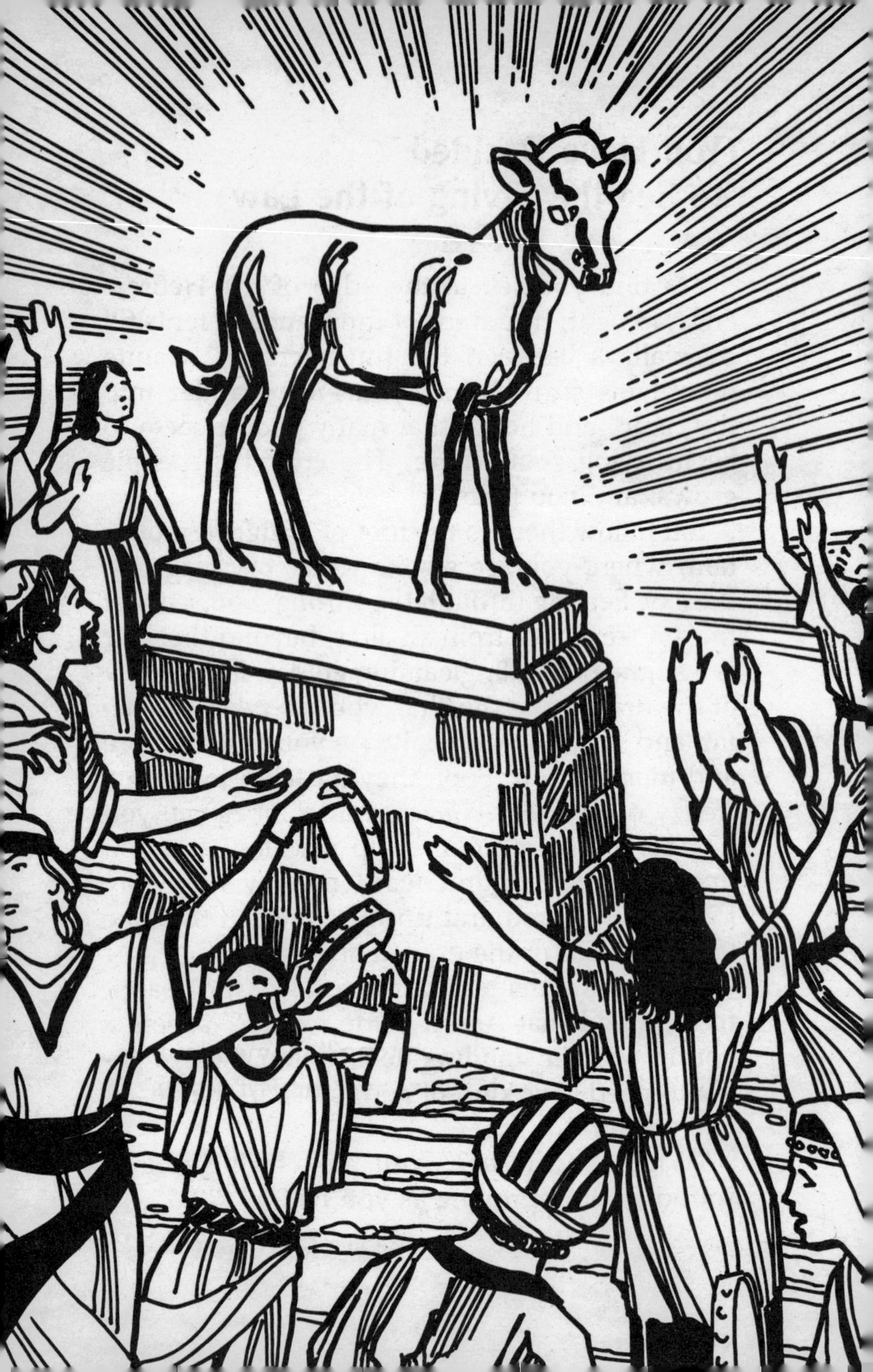

The young woman laughs drunkenly, and shouts to the crowd, "He wants to know where Moses is!"

Roars of anger burst from everyone around you. You begin to be afraid; this crowd is dangerous!

"Moses our deliverer is dead or gone—and good riddance, I say!" snarls a man. "I want no more to do with him or his God."

A chorus of agreements answer him.

Carefully, you edge your way to the back of the crowd. As soon as you think they have forgotten you, you begin to slip away. Suddenly, something draws your attention to the huge mountain behind the statue of the bull. Squinting through the smoke, you think you can see a lone figure standing there, about three-fourths of the way down the mountain. You walk quietly around the edge of the crowd, trying to get in position to have a better look.

"Look up there," someone close to you mutters, "I thought he was dead—he's been gone for forty days!"

More and more people begin to peer at the solitary figure on the mountain, and the noise of drunken revelry begins to quieten.

"What is that he is carrying?" someone asks. "The way he is stooped, you'd think it was solid rock!"

"Moses!" someone else shouts, and the crowd becomes deathly still. You wonder how these people can have forgotten so quickly the plagues of Egypt, what happened at the passover, and at the Red Sea, how they have been miraculously fed with quail and manna and given fresh water to drink—and most of this within the three months since they left Egypt!

All eyes are now on Moses. He stands on the edge of a cliff, surveying the scene before him. Suddenly, with a roar of rage, he lifts the stone tablets high above his head and hurls them down to the foot of the mountain. Leaping swiftly down the space remaining between them, Moses strides over to the golden bull. Seizing it furiously, he throws it in to a blazing fire.

In a voice filled with rage and pain, Moses speaks to Aaron, "What did these people do to you, that you led them into such great sin?"

Before Aaron begins to answer, you see the chariot appear behind an outcropping of rock. Although you are curious about what will happen next, you are glad to leave this time, for it has been dangerous and uncomfortable.

You climb into the chariot with relief, and take the reins in your hands.

Go to page 84.

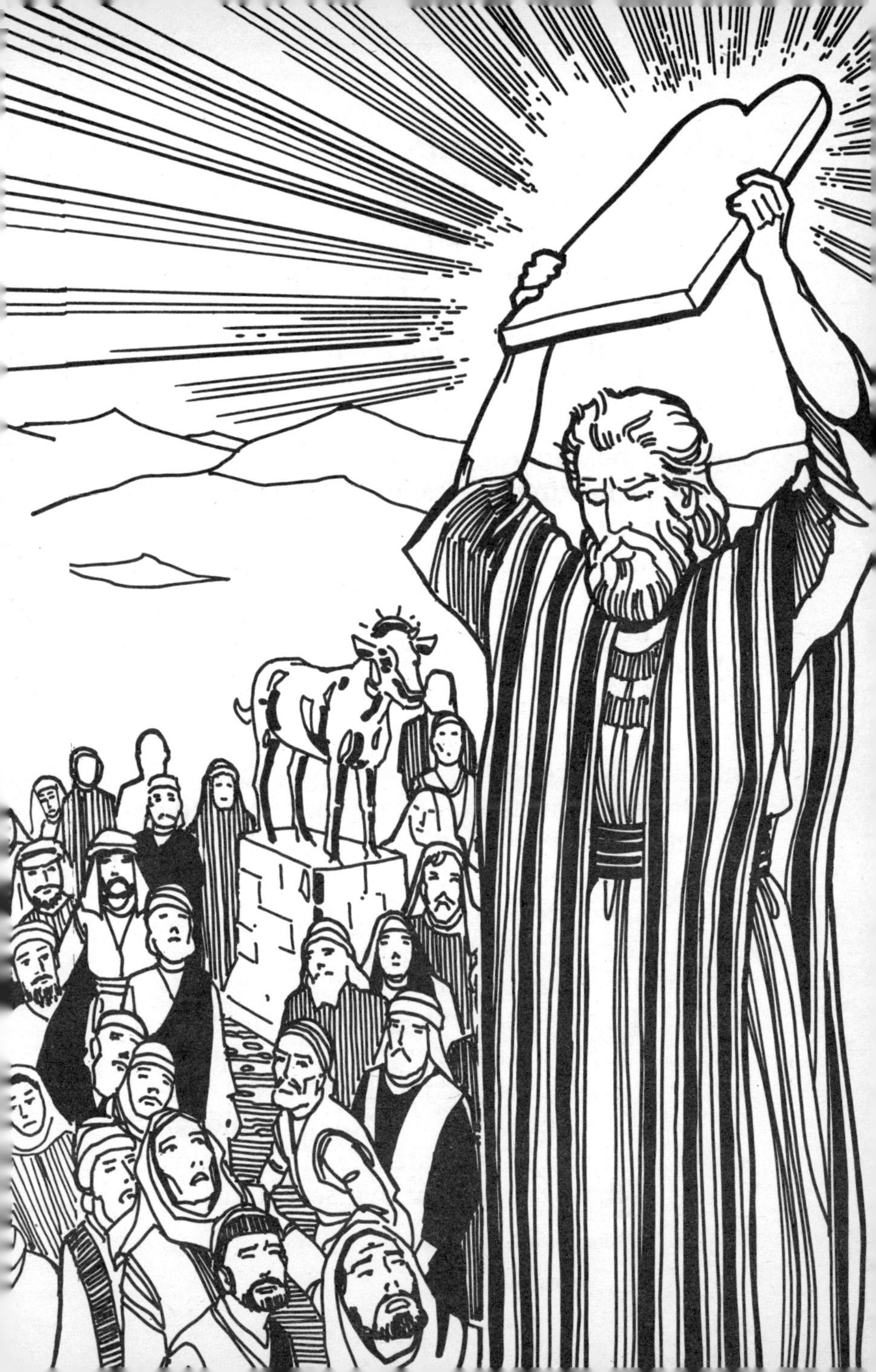

(You Have Decided to Trust the Egyptian)

You hope that this kind-looking man is not going to take you back to the place of horror, where you saw the old man being so cruelly whipped. You're sure that the baby in the basket *must* have been Moses, in spite of the boy denying the name. But it is too late to follow now, as the Egyptian has a strong hand on your shoulder, and is propelling you along with him as he walks. You realize with a start that he is speaking to you, and expects an answer.

"I'm sorry, I didn't hear you," you stammer uneasily. The man stares at you curiously, yet not unkindly.

"Whatever is the matter with you, boy?" He slaps you playfully and tousles your hair roughly. "Where did you come from that you're as pale as the mists that rise from our goddess, the Nile?"

You continue to walk beside him, thinking furiously. You decide to ignore his question, and try to find out who the slaves are.

"Who are the slaves I saw by the river, sir?" you ask, hoping your voice is polite and that he doesn't notice you never answered his question about where you have come from.

"Why, I thought everyone knew, although it isn't a pretty sight to watch, is it? I've always been glad that I'm not their overseer; I just don't have the stomach for whipping old men!" The Egyptian glances at you briefly, and continues walking briskly.

"The pharaoh has need of many bricks, you know, for building—and we're almost overrun with Apiru and other foreigners. So they make the bricks and we keep them out of trouble. That way the Pharaoh has enough bricks, and need not fear that these foreigners will have the time or the courage to make mischief. Understand?"

"Yes," you answer slowly, "but where do the Apiru come from—why are they here?"

"That's an easy question, boy—they've been here for four-hundred years or so, although there are a *lot* more of them now than there used to be. Some call them Hebrews. They are a people from some dusty country far away from here. They're trouble, though, I can tell you. Just imagine thinking there is only *one* god—what a ridiculous idea! As to why they're here, that's a very long story." The Egyptian stops walking suddenly, and faces you, putting both hands on your shoulders. "But what am I to do with you, eh boy?"

Go to page 26.

(You Have Decided to Run Away to Find the Chariot)

"Thanks for everything," you call over your shoulder, as you wheel about and take off at a fast jog. Hapu shouts something that you cannot hear, but you keep your steps steady and even, heading in the direction—you hope—of the river. The daylight is just melting into dusk, and you notice that the desert air grows cooler fast; you find that you are uncomfortably chilly, as well as exhausted and hungry.

You keep running down the strange streets, the statues looming ominously in unexpected places. You find yourself now on an unpaved, dusty road; you strain to hear the familiar sound of light wind through the reeds by the river's edge. At last you are past the last houses on the road, your steps slowing now from almost-total exhaustion. The moon has not yet risen, and the night sky is ink-black. Stars hang suspended from the velvet heavens. There are no familiar sounds, and your steps falter to a stop. You are completely alone, in a strange time and a strange place.

You stand there, frozen with the enormity of being so totally isolated from everything familiar. There is no sign of your chariot—and you have the feeling that it is not going to appear like magic, just because you want it to.

With a tired sigh, you turn your steps back in

the direction from which you have come. You realize that you will have to return to Hapu's house—if you are lucky enough to find it. You only hope that he'll let you in, after you ran away. Weary and discouraged, you wonder if you'll ever finish your quest.

Suddenly, you realize that you've only finished your first day; everything will look better tomorrow. With a lift in your spirits, you see Hapu's house just ahead; Hapu himself is outlined in the light of the doorway, peering anxiously down the street. With a glad shout, he welcomes you, and you realize that you don't feel nearly so alone anymore.

Hapu leads you up a narrow stairway, and into a small room. Two thick mats are ready on the floor, blankets folded neatly at the foot of the mat.

"I thought you must be awfully hungry, so I saved some food for you," Hapu says with a smile, as he hands you a flat loaf of bread, some cheese, and a large cup of cool, delicious water. Never has anything tasted so good. Gratefully, you smile your thanks as you devour supper.

"Thanks, Hapu," you say sincerely, "you're a good friend." You sink down on your mat thankfully, feeling yourself falling asleep almost before you can pull the rough blanket over yourself. It has been a very long day.

Go to page 29.

(You Have Decided to See What Moses Sees)

The chariot vanishes silently. You glance swiftly around to take stock of your surroundings—your heart thuds uncomfortably as you realize you are clinging precariously to the sheer rock face of an immensely high mountain. As far around as you can see, jagged tops jut into the sky like huge, jumbled teeth. Gusts of wind tear mercilessly at you, almost plucking you from your place. You grit your teeth, and squint into the swirling dust dancing off the rock face.

A flash of motion attracts your attention. You peer through stinging lids at a solitary figure, picking his way carefully through the maze of craggy boulders. You recognize Moses, following a faintly-discernible path up the mountain. Your fingers cling desperately to depressions in the rocks, you shift your feet slowly to find a wider ledge upon which to stand. Creeping cautiously, inch by inch, your feet find a less precarious hold. Moses—and the path—are just ahead of you. Still the wind tears at you as you make your way toward more solid ground.

At last you stumble gratefully onto the path. Moses is only a few feet away. You stop for just a moment to let your wildly beating heart slow a bit. Suddenly the wind ceases, and an eerie silence engulfs you and the entire mountain. The air around you seems to throb and pulsate with expectancy. Moses has disappeared around a massive boulder just ahead. The silence is so complete and so full that you almost cannot bear it—you find that you have dropped involuntarily to your knees, and now you stumble forward on all fours, your knees scraped and bleeding, toward Moses. You round the boulder, searching wildly for him.

Your eyes slide over the transfixed face of Moses to the object of his attention. A huge bush, clinging tenaciously to life in this rugged terrain, is ablaze with flames. There is no sound in the raging fire—huge tongues of fire curl in absolute silence. The tiny leaves of the bush tremble ever so slightly, their glossy deep green undimmed and untouched by the flames. Now you know what is meant by the deafening silence—your ears throb painfully, and you find that you are gasping for breath. You cannot take your eyes from the blazing bush, which shudders in the ecstasy of the holy fire.

Your senses whirl, and you wonder dazedly if you are fainting—a bright white mist suddenly blots everything from sight. Gasping in relief, you realize that you are slumped on the floor of

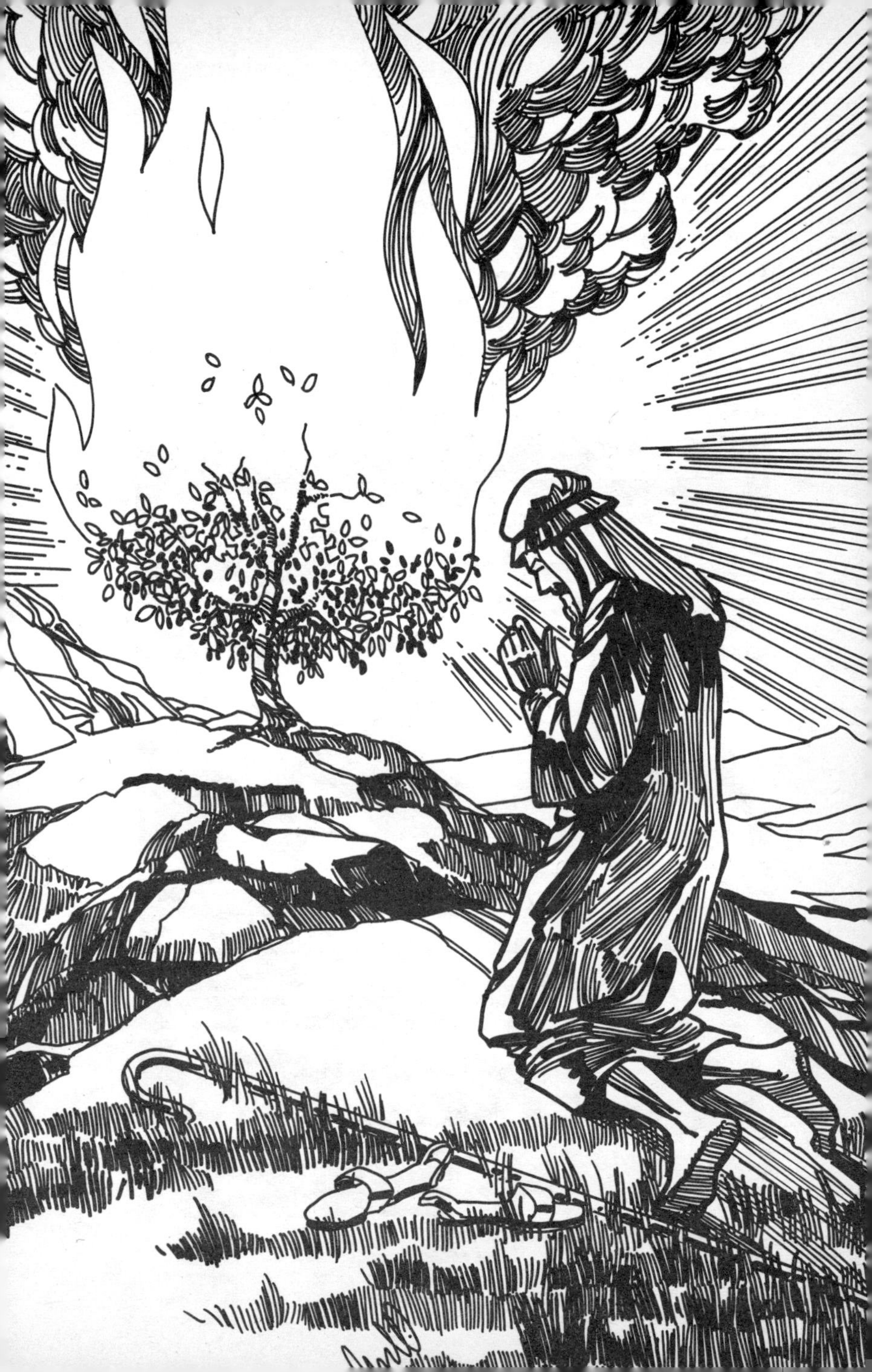

the chariot. The gentle, clear voice of the steed chimes bell-like in your ears.

"You could not have stood much more, little one," the steed says softly. "The presence of God's Spirit is powerful and awesome. Now I will take you just a little forward, to see Moses preparing to return to Egypt."

You take the reins gratefully in your hands and wait for the transition.

Go to page 107.

(The Passover)

"Go swiftly to your homes now," says Moses urgently, "for the Angel of Death is already abroad in the land. Give thanks to our Lord for our deliverance, and be ready to leave at a moment's notice."

Quietly and quickly, some of the people slip out of the door and into the pitch-black night. The door closes behind them, and you notice that everyone here appears ready to leave; small bundles are at everyone's feet. There is something disquieting in the heavy, silent air. All eyes are open wide in fear and wonder; Moses is calm and steadfast.

"Remember the Lord's instructions for this night," says Moses. "Obey them as a lasting ordinance for you and your descendants. When you enter the land that the Lord will give you as He promised, observe this ceremony. And when your children ask you, 'What does this ceremony mean to you?' then tell them, 'It is the passover sacrifice to the Lord who passed over the houses of the Israelites in Egypt and spared our homes when He struck down the Egyptians.'"

You watch in awe as the passover meal is served. Together, you silently share the roasted meat, served with flat bread. No one feels like talking; you all eat until the meat is entirely gone. You know that this is the night of the passover—easy to read about, but not so easy to get through. A sense of mortal dread presses down heavily like a real presence in the room—you have never been so frightened in your life. Only Moses looks confident and calm.

The man beside you raises his head expectantly. "The hour of midnight is here," he says quietly. "Listen."

You strain your ears for any sound, but at first hear nothing. Then, far in the distance, you hear a piercing wail. The wail grows louder, and is joined by other tortured laments. The cries build, making you feel that you are going mad with terror; closer and closer comes the awful sound. The Angel of Death is nearing. Those around you have sunk to their knees in prayer, their lips moving soundlessly. Your heart is pounding, as you also fall to your knees.

The wails begin anew, and you can tell that they are coming from the Egyptian houses just beyond the flimsy Hebrew homes. You hold your breath and wait—time stands still. The faces around you are pale, and the hands clasped in prayer are white-knuckled and shaking. The presence of death makes you almost faint with dread.

After what seems like an eternity of waiting, another shriek of despair slices into the terrible silence—yet this awful cry comes from the other side of the Hebrew homes. The heart-wrenching screams continue, now fading into the distance. Death has indeed passed over this house. You are filled with awe, as the thought of what has really happened here tonight sinks deep into your heart. You will never forget this night as long as you live.

All around you, people rise from their knees, terror and joy mingled in their faces. None of you will ever be quite the same again, for the power of the Almighty has touched each life. The next few hours until dawn pass in a blur.

A sudden urgent knock at the door startles everyone. Moses speaks with someone outside, and after a low word with his family, leaves the house. In a short while, Moses returns. "Make haste," he says quietly, "for Pharaoh has commanded us to leave. We are to take our flocks and our herds, and go."

Everyone around you picks up his or her bundle; the air is electric with excitement. The children of Israel have been delivered from their captivity.

You all move out into the street, which is crowded with people now; everyone is buzzing delightedly with excitement. There is tremendous confusion, as people mix with flocks of animals, and tired children wail. Terrified Egyptians appear, their arms loaded with items of gold and silver.

"Take our treasures, please," they beg, "but go

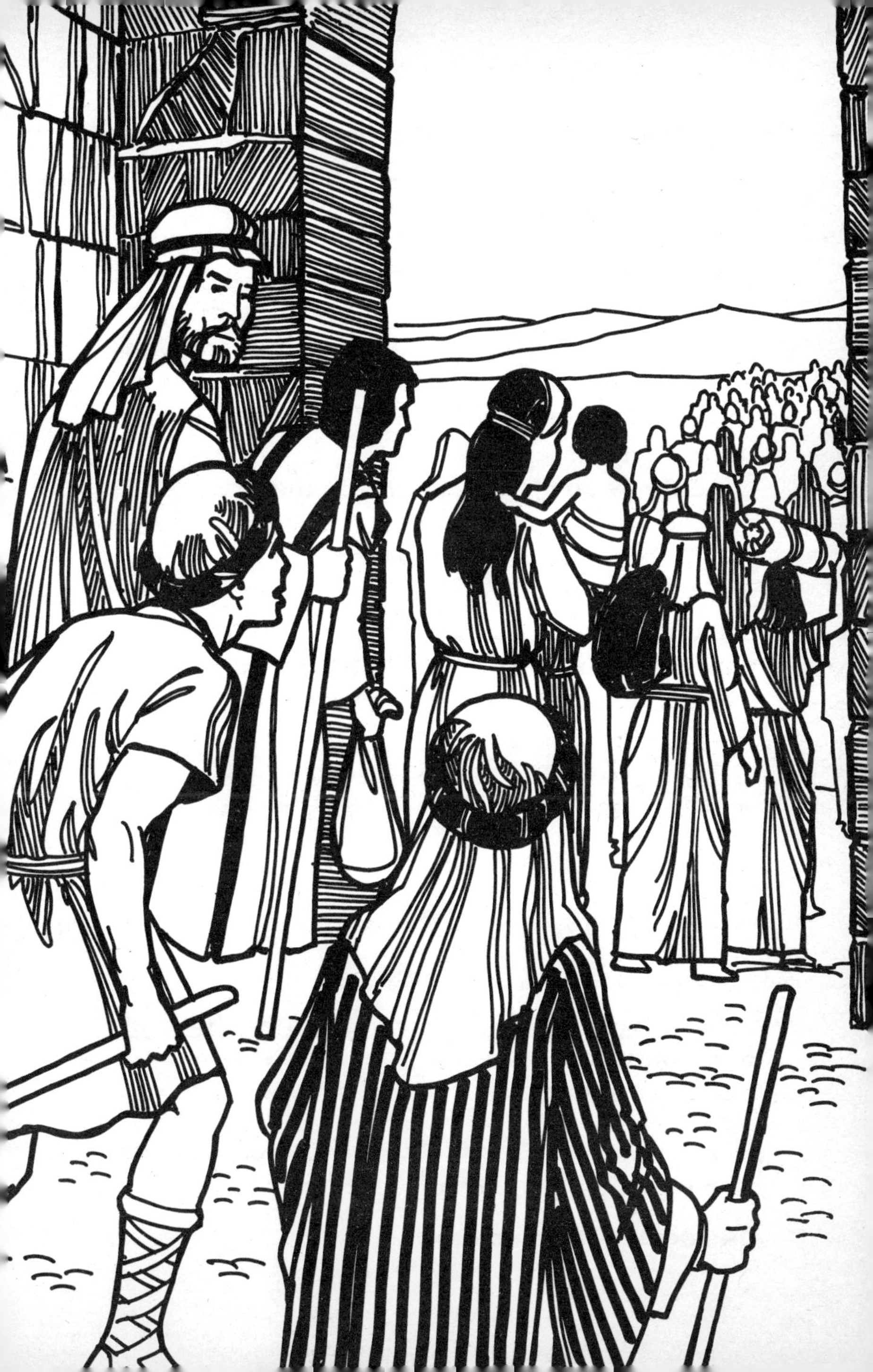

quickly away from our land!"

All over the city, more and more people crowd into the streets; the confusion increases. All are looking to Moses for guidance. The journey to the promised land is about to begin.

You see out of the corner of your eye that the chariot waits for you behind a reed hut, and you move quietly to step inside. The voice comes to you softly through the din of confusion in the street beyond.

"You may go forward in time to the crossing of the Red Sea, or forward to the time of the dedication of the tabernacle; the choice is entirely yours."

You know that both events are important; you really do not know which time you should choose. You take the reins in your hand, and think carefully.

If you decide to see the crossing of the Red Sea, go to page 135.

If you decide to see the tabernacle, go to page 122.

(You Have Decided to Go Inside Hapu's House)

Exhausted, and not certain that you have done the right thing, you manage a tired smile; Hapu delightedly ushers you through the door. You find yourself in a spacious hall, where an older woman smiles a welcome. Hapu introduces you to his mother, who leads you both down a wide corridor to what you fervently hope is going to be the kitchen.

To your surprise, you enter a small but comfortable room, furnished with couches and tables. Hapu eagerly sits on the floor by a low table, upon which is an enormous bowl of melon, and another of small, flat loaves of bread. He beckons you to join him, his mouth already full. You do not wait to be invited twice, for you have discovered that you are hungrier than you ever thought possible. You sit down, and bite hungrily into the juicy melon; the bread is unlike anything you've eaten, but it is delicious.

"Soon, my father will be home," mumbles Hapu, his mouth full of the last bite of his bread. "Let's go out into the garden until he gets here." Hapu leads you back into the corridor, and out through a door at the end into a small, walled garden. It is not nearly as beautiful as the garden in the temple, but it is nice all the same. In the center, there is a small fountain, bubbling merrily. Here, too, there are palm trees, and fragrant jasmine. You both flop contentedly down on the cool stones at the fountain's base, and stretch out, flat and relaxed.

"Your home is very nice," you tell Hapu, who smiles proudly. You are surprised that the house is so comfortable—you had always thought that all Egyptians who were not royalty were peasants or slaves who lived in mud huts. "What job does your father do?"

"Well, he used to be a scribe in Pharaoh's court. But since he was a boy, he has been very gifted in carving. One day, before I was born, Pharaoh saw some of my father's work and liked it so much that he gave my father a new job. So now he is a craftsman for Pharaoh." Hapu's voice is warm with pride.

You both lapse into contented silence, the musical murmur of the fountain pleasant and lulling. "After we have greeted my father, we must go to sleep," Hapu's voice jars you from your comfortable almost-doze. You stumble to your feet as Hapu leaps to his, running to the Egyptian man who has just entered the small garden.

"Well, boy—how did you like the best school in the land?" he asks you kindly.

"It's very nice," you reply politely, "and I thank you very much for letting me be a guest in your home. Hapu has been very kind. But if you please, I don't know what your name is, sir."

The Egyptian shakes his head with amusement. "Of course you don't—how stupid of me. It's Semnet. Now off to sleep with both of you—the sun rises early tomorrow!"

Hapu leads you up a narrow stairway, and into a small room. Two thick mats are ready on the floor, and you throw yourself down onto the mat gratefully. Almost before you pull the rough blanket over yourself, you realize you are falling asleep. It has been quite a day.

Hours later, you wake with moonlight streaming into the window. You hear Hapu's quiet breathing on the other mat, and you get up carefully, so as not to wake him. You feel refreshed, and ready to get on with your quest. You really don't want another day of school tomorrow, for you don't see how that could possibly help. You look out of the window at the sleeping city, hoping to see the chariot of fire—but you see nothing. Should you go outside and search for it, or should you just go back to sleep and figure things out in the morning?

If you decide to go back to sleep, turn to page 29.

If you decide to search for the chariot, turn to page 18.

(Through the Streets)

You walk slowly through a total darkness unlike any night you have ever seen. You are grateful for Semnet's whispered directions, for you know you would never be able to find Moses' house without help. You find yourself breathing carefully, so different is the air you breathe. You look neither right nor left, but keep Semnet's directions in your mind, and follow them carefully.

Presently, you find yourself turning into a narrow street of reed houses, flimsy and small. Here, every house has the mark of blood above the doorway. Carefully, you count the houses until you at last reach the one that Semnet has told you is the house of Moses. You knock softly, and wait.

The door opens, and a man beckons you in with a smile. Many people are crammed into the reed hut; you recognize one of Moses' sons, and edge your way toward him. It is almost midnight, and you wonder what is going to happen next; everyone here seems to be expectant. Moses enters, closing the door behind him. The crowd inside the house is silent, waiting for him to speak.

Go to page 59.

(You Have Decided to Stay in Egypt)

You are pretty certain that you know what happens in Midian, so you think you should remain here in Egypt to try to find some answers. Did Moses just kill the Egyptian overseer? Is the witness of his deed going to tell the authorities? Is this why God will not allow Moses to actually enter the promised land?

Suddenly, you notice that as you have been thinking, the chariot has disappeared. You decide to return to Semnet's home—until you remember that you are a number of years in the future. You wander uncertainly along the road, which follows the river's twisting course. The unmistakable reports of a whip's cracks assault your ears. *Are there slave-drivers everywhere in this country?* you wonder angrily. You glance toward the river and see the familiar sight of slaves working in the mud pits, driven on by overseers. You notice that here, the overseer is not actually beating anyone—he cracks his whip above their heads. The slaves are working well, and are allowed to stop briefly to sip water from a gourd cup, held for them by an old lady carrying a bucket.

Apparently, the old woman has finished her

task, for she abruptly leaves the mud pit, and hurries up the bank to the road. She looks tired, so you decide to offer her some help.

"May I carry that bucket for you, ma'am?" you ask her courteously.

"Thank you, young man," she answers you with a shaky smile. "We do not find many young Egyptian men as kind as you."

You are startled at being mistaken for an Egyptian, and can think of nothing to say; you fall into step beside her. Perhaps she can answer some questions for you.

"Do you live far from here?" you ask. You'd like to ask her if she knows about Moses, but you don't know how to begin.

"Not so far, young man—you are welcome to step in for some refreshment, if you would not be too proud to accept hospitality from a Hebrew," she answers, with a sidelong smile.

You feel embarrassed, and you find that you would like this lady to know that you are *not* an Egyptian oppressor—but you know that you can't reveal your quest.

"I would be honored to be a guest in your home," you answer honestly.

You and she walk in companionable silence for a while, and at last turn down a narrow little street, lined on both sides with flimsy huts made from bulrushes. The woman pushes open the thin door, and bids you enter before her. You find yourself in a very small, but surprisingly cheery house. She takes the bucket from you, and invites you to sit upon one of the mats on the earthen floor. She hands you a cup of cool water, and a little flat fruitcake; then she sits down beside you with an encouraging smile.

You thank her for her hospitality, then ask, "How can you be so cheerful and kind, when the Egyptians have made you a slave?" You think that in her place, you'd never give anything to a person you thought was an Egyptian!

The old lady smiles quietly. "We may be slaves, but no one can ever imprison our spirits. He-Who-Has-No-Name has chosen us as His people, and He will send us a deliverer in His own good time. It is an honor to be a Hebrew."

"Well," you answer slowly, "He'll have to send a deliverer pretty fast, won't He? I mean, your people can't exactly be thriving under the whip!"

Again, the lady smiles gently. "He will deliver us when He chooses. We have had many sorrows, but He hears our cries. I remember many years ago, when the pharaoh was very worried about how many Hebrews there were. He was afraid that we would revolt; so he gave the order that all our boy babies should be thrown into the river, and drowned. Most of our people believed then that He-Who-Has-No-Name had abandoned us; but I have always known that He keeps His promises. He will send us a deliverer, young man—you'll see!"

You feel very humble in the presence of such

Decide Your Own Adventure 73

faith; all you can do is thank her profusely for her kindness. She pats you gently as she leads you to the door of the hut. "Remember what I say, young Egyptian," she says as you take your leave, "and watch for Him to deliver us from bondage. Perhaps young Moses is the one chosen—have you heard of him?"

Electrified, you turn back to her. "Yes, I have! Why do you think he may be the one?" you ask urgently.

"Everyone is whispering that Prince Moses is by birth a Hebrew, and that today he has killed an Egyptian overseer. That is a crime punishable by death, on the pharaoh's order. Perhaps this is the beginning, or perhaps not. We will see." The lady waves a cheerful farewell, and you turn thoughtfully down the street.

You are so deep in thought that you almost do not notice the chariot waiting patiently for you at the end of the street. Still marveling at the strength of such faith, you climb slowly into the blazing chariot. Mechanically, you take the reins into your hands, and hear the voice tell you that at the next stop, you will find yourself still in Egypt, but about forty years into the future. You realize that in forty years or so, Moses will have returned from Midian. *This is going to be interesting!* you think in excitement. You pull the reins taut.

Turn to page 93.

(You Have Come to See Moses Bring Water From a Rock)

Through leaping flames you can dimly make out Hebrew tents, but you remain in the chariot. *This has never happened before!* you think in astonishment.

"There is something you should know, little one," says the voice of the steed softly. "You have come approximately thirty-eight years forward in time. All Hebrews who were over the age of twenty when the Lord God led them out of Egypt are now dead, save for Joshua, Caleb, and Moses."

"All?" you question in amazement.

"All," replies the steed gently. "The Lord God brought them to the very borders of the promised land in less than two years from the time they left Egypt. They had witnessed His mighty power in delivering them from captivity. They had been led by His guiding hand through the Red Sea and across the desert. They had been fed, given water to drink, and delivered to the promised land, yet time and time again they rebelled against Him. This time, rather than trust in Him to protect them in the land He had led them to, they chose to believe the false report of ten of the twelve men who had spied out the land. For this reason, the Lord condemned them to wander—one year in the wilderness for each day spent spying out Caanan—until every grumbling, disbelieving one of them was dead."

"Wait a minute," you puzzle. "If everyone over the age of twenty died during forty years of wandering"—you calculate silently, knowing that there were at least one million people—"then more than eighty people died every day for forty years!"

"That is correct," answers the voice gravely. "Do you think the judgement a harsh one?"

"No," you answer thoughtfully, "because the younger generation might have been led away from the Lord by their parents' rebellion.

"You have answered wisely," chimes the voice. "You are learning well, little one. Now it is time for you to see what you have come to see."

The dancing flames disappear, and the chariot vanishes.

The tents of the Hebrews cover the desert floor as far as the eye can see—and you are astonished all over again at the sheer number of people that Moses is leading. You break into an easy jog toward the center of the encampment, for you know that reaching the middle of such a multitude will not be the work of a few minutes. If you are *ever* to successfully complete your quest, you must find the answer to why Moses will not be allowed to enter the promised land. Perhaps the answer lies here, in this barren wilderness.

At last you reach the center; your dry mouth aches, and you chest is heaving. A large group of people are assembled nearby, and as you come closer, you are able to hear what they are saying.

"If only we had died when our brothers fell dead before the Lord," wails someone.

Complaining again, you think to yourself as you look for Moses. As you anxiously scan the crowd, you see Moses appear, framed in the doorway of his tent.

Another whining voice assails your ears, "Why did you bring us out of Egypt into this desert, that we and our livestock should die here?"

Now voices clamor, all filled with complaint: "Why did you bring us to this terrible place? It has no grain or figs, grapevines or pomegranates. And there is no water to drink!"

You watch Moses stride from his tent, beckoning Aaron to follow him. They walk swiftly through the crowd, which parts for them unwillingly. Their steps take them straight to the entrance to the tabernacle, where they prostrate themselves, face down. The grumbling people look away from the tabernacle uneasily, their complaints stilled for the moment.

You feel uneasy too, wondering what will happen next. In a very short time, you hear the blasts from the silver trumpet that summon the tribes to the tent of meeting. You hurry toward the tabernacle, hoping to find a good vantage point from which to watch.

Moses and Aaron stand at the entrance, waiting for the people to assemble. Before the entire community, the two stride a few steps, stopping in front of a large rock. Moses is holding a staff; he raises the staff, and in a strong voice, says, "Listen, you rebels, must *we* bring you water out of this rock?" Striking the rock twice with the staff, Moses steps back.

Water pours from the rock! Great shouts of excitement come from the crowd now! Once again, the people have forgotten that only moments before, they were furious with Moses. You notice that you hear no voices praising the Lord; instead, they are delighted with the power of Moses' words.

People rush forward to drink the clear water; soon they are bringing livestock too. Still you hear no one praising the power of the almighty God. *Something isn't quite right about this*, you think to yourself.

Thoughtfully, you walk back in the direction you came from. Even from this distance, you can see the chariot shimmering as it waits for you. You can't quite put your finger on what was wrong with the scene you just saw. Absentmindedly, you climb into the waiting chariot. You take the reins in your hands. Clearly and quietly, the voice says, "It is now time for you to go to the very end of Moses' journey."

Go to page 111.

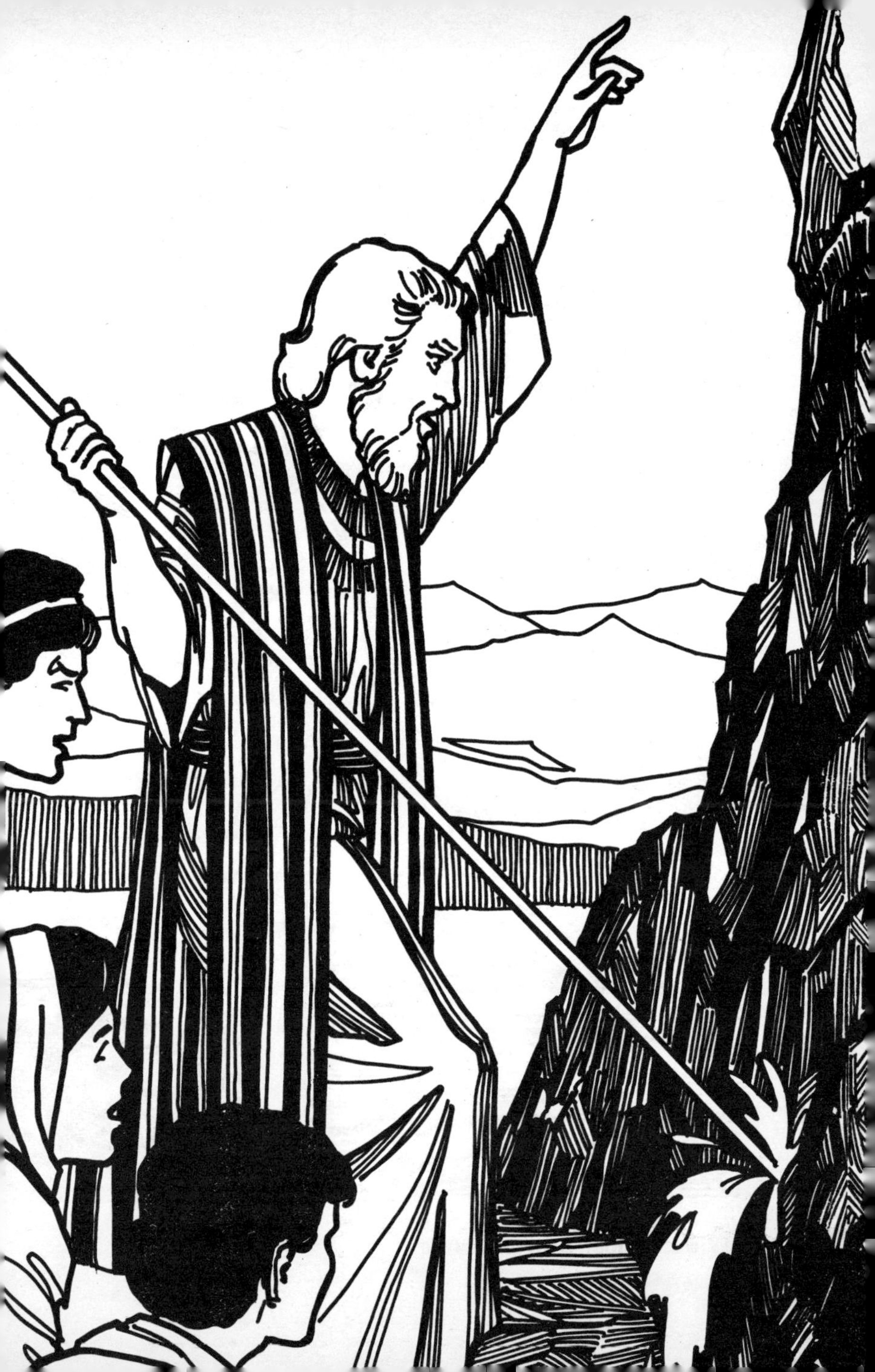

(You Take the Suggestion)

Somehow, your steed seems to know your decision without your having to speak. You pull the smooth leather of the reins taut, and suddenly find yourself on a hill overlooking the river.

At the water's edge, an Egyptian overseer is brutally beating an old man. You can see from here that the poor man can't possibly take much more beating—he is painfully thin, and his cries for mercy are weak and spent. Blood covers his head and back; he ceases to move or to cry out, but still the Egyptian beats him.

You are frantically trying to think of some way that you can help him, when you hear the sound of a galloping horse approaching. As the horse and rider rush wildly into sight, you see a young man throw himself from the animal and you hear his cry of rage as he attacks the Egyptian overseer with fists driven by fury.

The fight is uneven. The overseer is unused to defending himself, and is powerless unless he is whipping those who cannot fight back. The young man fights fiercely, and soon the overseer falls heavily, apparently striking his head on a large rock. The young man bends immediately to give his attention to the frail, broken, old man on the ground. He fills his cupped hands with water for the old man to drink, and begins gently washing the wounds with a cloth he has dipped in the river. "Thank you, my son," you hear the old man whisper. "The overseer would have killed me soon. But I fear that he is dead—if anyone hears of this, you will be in terrible trouble."

You crouch lower and glance quickly around. To your horror, you see that on the other side of the river, a man stands silently watching. You have no idea when he appeared or how much he may have seen. The fighter stands quickly, for he, too, has caught sight of the man. The man turns quickly on his heel, and vanishes over the ridge of the hill.

The young man quickly buries the overseer in a shallow grave in the sand. Then he picks up the injured slave and carries him gently to the waiting horse. He lays him on the animal carefully, then mounts. Unhurried, he turns the horse back in the direction from which he came. His back is straight and proud as he guides the animal slowly down the road. *He is probably being careful not to hurt the poor old man any more than is neces-*

sary, you think. If this is Moses, and you are pretty certain that it is, you like him already.

The chariot appears on your left—you are not even startled this time. You walk slowly toward it, thinking over what you have seen. Once again, the voice makes itself heard, "You may travel into the future to Midian if you choose, or you may remain in Egypt to see what happens to Moses next. The choice is entirely up to you."

You climb into the chariot, thinking carefully, and taking the reins into your hands.

**If you decide
to go to Midian, turn to page 37.**

**If you decide
to stay in Egypt, turn to page 70.**

(You Have Come to See the Spies Return)

You find yourself in a large and beautiful oasis—in the midst of the vast Hebrew encampment. Although desert can be seen on the horizon in all directions, here palm trees sway gently in the soft breezes. You hear the familiar bleat of goats and sheep. Around you, clusters of people are so busy talking that they do not notice your arrival in their midst.

"They arrived about an hour ago," you hear someone near your elbow say. You turn, and find that you are at the edge of a large group of excited people.

"By my count, they have been gone forty days," he continues. "I saw them as they entered camp, and they were heavily laden with magnificent fruits."

You decide to risk seeming incredibly stupid, and murmur, "Who?"

Several people stare at you curiously. The man who has been speaking looks at you in reproach. "The twelve men sent by Moses to explore Canaan, of course. Where are your brains, lad?" Before you can think of an answer, another voice speaks.

"Moses surely will call us soon to the tent of meeting, to tell us what they report. We had better go now so we can get close enough to hear what he says." There is excited agreement, and the crowd moves away. You decide to follow, as they wind their way through the tents toward the tabernacle in the center. Along the way, people around you discuss the situation.

One man asks hopefully, "If our spies did bring back magnificent fruit, doesn't that prove that the land is as wonderful as we have been promised?"

"Of course," answers his companion, "but why would such a bountiful land be uninhabited? And if it is inhabited, don't you imagine that those who live there will fight to the death to keep it?"

"You may be certain of that!" responds a third man forcefully. "Moses has probably brought us all this way only to be killed by the inhabitants of this so-called 'promised land'!"

All around, a grumble of agreement begins. Suddenly, the clear voice of a boy about your own age rings out.

"Why would God allow that?" he questions. "He didn't allow us to die at the hands of Pharaoh's army." All within earshot grow silent. The boy continues. "God has not allowed us to die of hunger, or of thirst—in fact," he laughs, "God isn't even allowing our shoes to wear out!"

The crowd is momentarily quiet. *Well,* you think, *that's exactly what I was wondering! How much does God have to do for these people before they will trust Him?*

"Quiet, boy!" roars one of the men. "You know nothing of war! You leave the planning of this battle—for there is sure to be one—to your elders!"

The boy catches your eye and you both shrug as if to say, "What can we do?" By this time, your group has been joined by many others, all heading in the same direction. You are now within sight of the tabernacle but the crowd around it is deep. Straining to see, you can barely make out Moses, and a group of travel-worn men with him.

As the immense throng quietens, one of the men with Moses begins to speak.

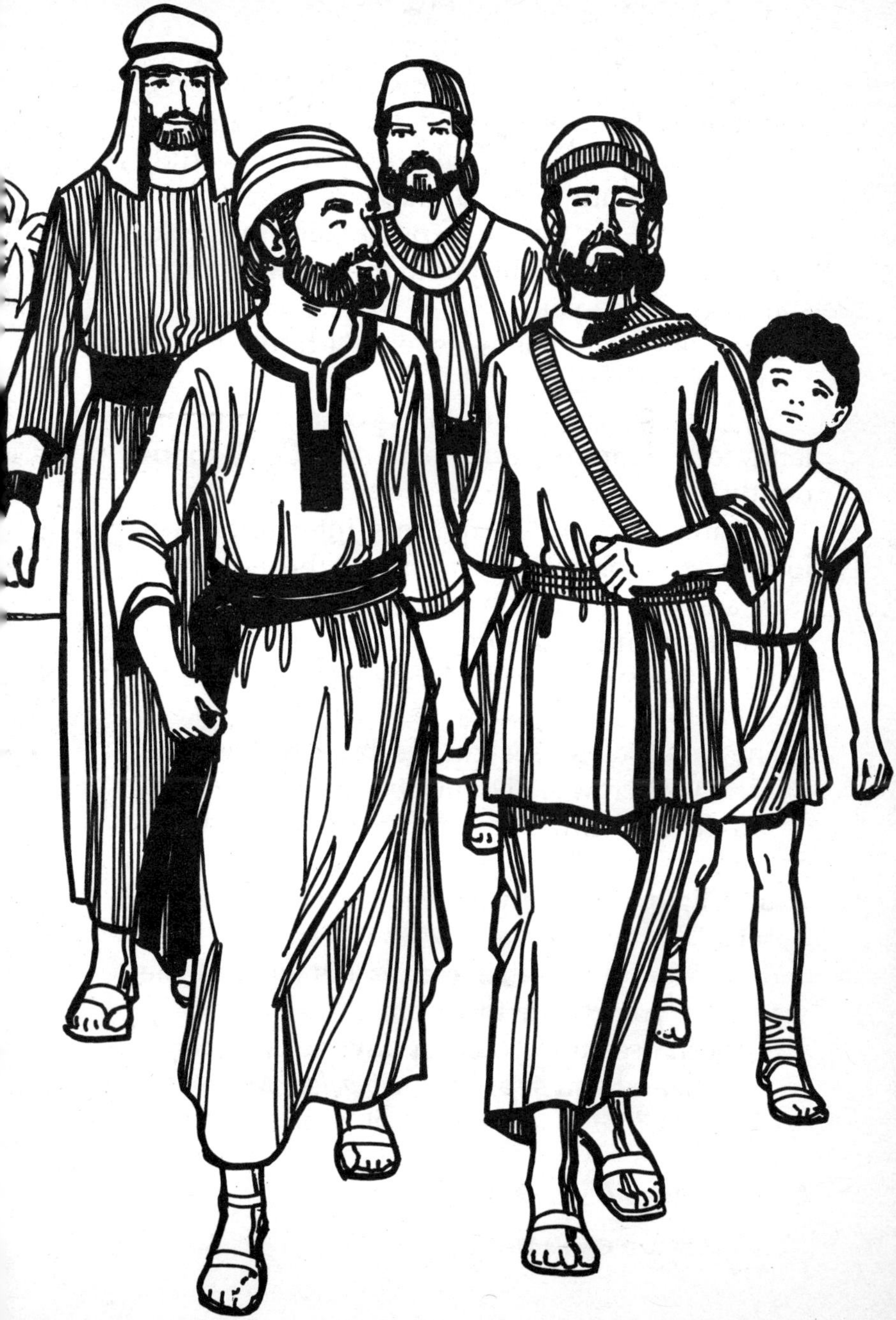

"We went into the land to which you sent us, and it does flow with milk and honey! Here is its fruit. But the people who live there are powerful, and the cities are fortified and very large."

Another of the twelve steps forward to speak. "Who is that?" you whisper to the young woman standing beside you.

"That is Caleb," she whispers, "I think he is a friend of Joshua."

"We should go up and take possession of the land, for we can certainly do it," says Caleb confidently.

Yet another of the explorers interrupts in a loud, angry voice, "We can't attack those people; they are stronger than we are!"

An angry murmur spreads through the fearful crowd. "I heard that all the people who live in that land are giants," one man mutters.

The voice of Moses carries bravely over the loud, angry crowd. "Do not be terrified; do not be afraid of them. The Lord your God, who is going before you, will fight for you, as He did for you in Egypt, before your very eyes, and in the desert. There you saw how the Lord your God carried you, as a father carries his son, all the way until you reached this place."

It doesn't seem to you that anyone is listening to Moses, and you slip away. *How does Moses ever get this bunch to do anything?* you wonder.

Go to page 75.

(You Have Decided to Stay With Moses)

As quickly as the decision is made, you find yourself on a narrow street; the houses here are made of reeds. You are certain that these must be some of the Hebrew homes. Hesitating, for you are uncertain of what your next move should be, you stand still for a moment, looking around you.

You hear many voices behind you, and turn in their direction. A large group of Hebrew slaves, all talking and gesturing excitedly, moves toward you. You blend easily into their group, and listen.

"But listen to this!" one of the Hebrews shouts excitedly. "Moses did even more than that! Even the overseers are frightened to death—the Egyptian gods will not serve them now! This is what I heard," he continues.

"Even after all the plagues that the Lord has sent upon the Egyptians, still Pharaoh told Moses that we would not be allowed to leave! *And* Pharaoh said that the next time he saw Moses' face, Moses would die. Moses agreed that he would never see Pharaoh again, but tonight is the night that the Angel of Death is to pass through the land!"

"I know, I know! Are you ready?" chimes in another excited voice.

"Yes, of course," chorus many voices.

"If you ask me," grumbled a surly-looking Hebrew, "all that Moses has brought us is trouble." Many of the crowd look at the speaker with horror, but others nod their agreement with him.

"Who made Moses our deliverer? If our God is so powerful, why have we been slaves here for longer than anyone can remember?" You are shocked to hear murmurs of agreement.

"Did not Moses cause us more trouble than we had before he came? When he told Pharaoh that we must be allowed to go out into the desert to worship our God, Pharaoh decided that we didn't have enough to do. Who can forget that we had to gather our own straw, while still making as many bricks as we had to before! He tells us, 'Do this, get ready for that!' so often that I'm sick with it! If Moses is our great deliverer, I'll stay here a slave, thank you!" the man roars in anger.

"And I'll tell you something else," he continues loudly. "I am not going to slaughter any passover lamb! The Angel of Death is no stranger to our house since we have been in bondage. There's not going to be anything special about tonight!"

You see men in the crowd glance at each other uneasily. "I may have my doubts about Moses," whispers one, "but I'll do what he says tonight, of all nights."

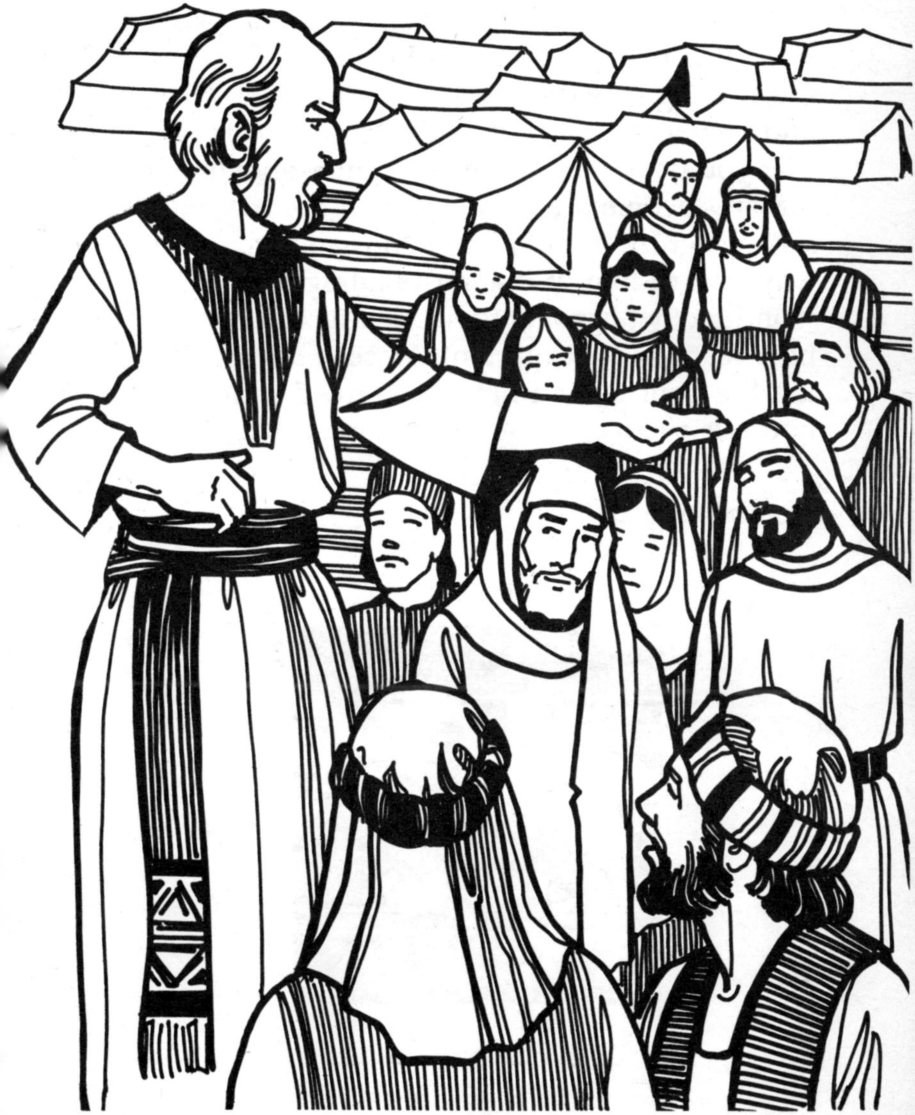

You slip easily out of the crowd, for you have heard enough. To your relief, you see Moses himself come quietly out of his house to talk to the waiting crowd. He spares you a brief smile, and beckons you into his tiny home. You are glad that you have found him, and enter gratefully.

Many people are crammed into the reed hut; you recognize one of Moses' sons and edge your way toward him. It is almost midnight, and you wonder what is going to happen next; everyone here seems to be expectant. Moses returns, closing the door behind him. The crowd inside the house is silent, waiting for him to speak.

Go to page 59.

(You Are Joining the Family of Semnet)

You find yourself deposited right on Semnet's street, several doors down from his home. It is odd to feel familiar and comfortable here, but you do. The sun has not yet set, and you are surprised that you see no one on the streets. There should be throngs of people, yet you are alone.

You stride quickly down the street, and knock briskly upon the door. You hope you will be accepted here—the last time you saw Semnet and Hapu was more than forty years ago! You hear footsteps advancing toward the door, and hold your breath anxiously.

The door opens a tiny crack, and someone peers cautiously out. Then the door is flung wide open, and Hapu—over fifty, but still easily-recognizable—pulls you hastily inside.

"I'm sorry to be so rude," Hapu says unhappily, "but with the world upside down in the judgement of the gods, one can't be too careful."

What on earth is he talking about? you wonder, as he nervously leads you down the corridor you remember so well, and out into the small garden. The fountain is still bubbling merrily, and the sweet smells still fill the air. You are delighted to see Semnet—an old man, but still obviously well--sitting by the fountain's edge.

"What has been happening?" you ask worriedly, as you notice that Semnet looks as alarmed as Hapu.

"Where have you been, boy?" says Semnet, looking at you curiously. "Have you not seen the gods of Egypt cast down, one by one?"

You answer carefully that you have been away, and have only just returned.

"Then sit down, have some refreshment, and let me tell you what has been happening," says Semnet. He seems frightened, yet strangely excited. You sit obediently beside him, and wait for him to speak.

"I have wondered for years if the Hebrew God might be more powerful than the gods of Egypt, but I said nothing. I have watched the Hebrews—many of them have amazing faith in spite of their slavery. They live and die in bondage, talking about their God, and their hope that He will send one to deliver them. Now such a deliverer may actually be here!" Semnet's voice rises in excitement. I have heard that a Hebrew called Moses visited the pharaoh's court recently, and that he performed greater acts of magic than any of Pharaoh's magicians. And," Semnet continues triumphantly, "he is demanding that Pharaoh let the Hebrew people go!"

"Well, I wish they were gone already," says Hapu nervously. "If it were up to me, I'd give them anything they wanted, just so they would leave!"

"But you still haven't told me what has been happening," you say slowly.

Semnet starts to speak, but is interrupted by Hapu. "It has been awful! First, our waters turned to blood. *All* our water—even that in our fountain. Hapu's eyes are dark pools of horror at the memory. He shudders as he continues, "I came here, to our garden and our beautiful laughing fountain, to escape from the terror outside." Beads of perspiration stand on his brow as he remembers, and his face drains of color. "The garden was silent as the tomb—no songs of birds, no drone of bees. And then I saw that our fountain ran red with blood!"

Hapu covers his anguished face with shaking hands. Semnet quietly takes up the tale. "You cannot imagine the foul smell, the filthy flies, and the raging thirst."

"Osiris did not help us," Semnet continues. "Fish and birds died, and the stench was everywhere—there was no escape. For seven days our water was a torrent of blood. This could only have been caused by the hand of the Hebrew God," Semnet says gently. "Only One more powerful than all of our gods could execute such a judgement. The pharaoh should have listened then, and let the Hebrews go, as Moses asked."

"Next came the plague of frogs," Hapu quavers. "Of course we were not to kill them—they

Decide Your Own Adventure **95**

are sacred to our gods. But you could not take a step without crushing at least one," he says, revulsion twisting his face. "The foul creatures were even in our cooking vessels and in our beds!"

"Then our great god of the earth, Geb, was shown powerless," Hapu continues. "Terrible fleas were everywhere—our animals suffered, as we did, and no magic would prevail against them. One by one, as my father says, our gods were cast down."

Semnet's face is grave. "The hail and fire were especially terrible to me," he says. His eyes were faraway, and the stark fear in them makes you shiver. "On a beautiful, cloudless day, huge boulders of hailstones suddenly rained down on our heads. There was panic in the streets, as people were knocked senseless by the pounding hail. Then great curling flames descended upon us, and the air was filled with screams and the roar of thousands of flames. Clothing leaped into fire, and the din of the huge hailstones striking the

Decide Your Own Adventure 97

earth was almost deafening. Everywhere was blood, and fire, and horror."

"To me, the boils were the most terrible," Hapu interrupts in a stricken whisper. "Of all nine plagues, the boils were the worst." He turns to you, his face ashen. "Did you have them?" he whispers. "Did you wake up one morning shrieking in pain, your body covered with oozing, stinking sores? Did you smell your flesh rotting, and watch the poison crawl over every square inch of your burning skin?"

You shrink away from Hapu instinctively, recoiling from his face frozen in icy terror. Your nerves are stretched to the snapping point.

The quiet voice of Semnet seems to come from a great distance. "We have heard it whispered that there is yet one more plague—the most terrible of all. The Hebrew God has declared through Moses that the firstborn male in every household will die—including even the firstborn male of all our livestock!"

Hapu's body is shuddering almost uncontrollably. Semnet's face is frightened, and yet strangely peaceful. He turns to you urgently. "Although this house will see death this night," Semnet whispers gently, "I am not afraid. I know now that the gods of the Egyptians are as dust under the feet of the God of the Hebrews. I place myself in His hands. But for you, my friend—the house of an Egyptian is no place for you this night."

Semnet propels you hurriedly to the door, as he gives you directions on how to find Moses' house. "Run swiftly now; seek the home of Prince Moses on this night."

Undecided, you hesitate at the open door.

"May He-Who-Has-No-Name protect you," Semnet's voice is low in your ear. "Run now—for the sun will set soon!"

Semnet's strong hands shove you forcibly into the quiet street. "Do not worry about me," he smiles, "Now that I know who is God, I am content. Go!"

You start slowly down the street, your steps quickening as you feel in the very air you breathe that something terrible is about to happen.

Go to page 69.

(Following Moses)

"Moses!" you call, your voice shaking.

He turns with a smile, waiting for you to reach him. He sits down with a weary sigh on an outcropping of rock, and beckons you to join him. You had been afraid that such a mighty man of God would be difficult to approach, but as you sit beside him you realize that you feel comfortable.

"Moses," you begin hesitantly, "I'm sorry to bother you now, but I just wondered . . ." you trail off, unsure of how to continue. You cast a sidelong glance at him, and see that he is patiently waiting.

"Why won't God let you enter the promised land?" the words tumble out. "You are the one who led the people here, why can't you cross the Jordan? It doesn't seem fair!" You have come to truly admire this man, and you don't see why the punishment must be so severe—whatever he did cannot have been so terrible.

Moses smiles gently. "It is time that I am finished with my labors. The Lord himself will show me this land that He has promised. I am not sad, my son. Why are you so angry?"

"Because it doesn't seem fair that you should be punished when you have struggled so hard for so many years!" you stammer furiously.

Moses puts a comforting arm around you. "There is a very good reason why I may not go with Israel into the land that God has promised us." He pauses, then asks kindly, "What do you think God's purpose has been in delivering the Hebrews from slavery in Egypt?"

You think carefully, then answer. "To lead Israel to a better life?"

"No, my son. We are His people; through us someday every nation will be blessed. The 'better life' will come when God's people are obedient to Him. We are to stand as a beacon to the whole earth, letting all see that there are no other gods before Him," Moses answers quietly.

"Who do you think sustained a whole nation of people for forty years in the wilderness? Who saw to it that neither clothing nor sandals wore out during that whole time? Who rained food down on us, and made sweet water to flow from rocks in the barren desert? Did I do all this, my son?" Moses' face is stern as he asks you these questions.

You feel humbled as you answer, "No, you did none of these things, Moses—God himself did."

Moses' face is gentler now, as he continues. "Yes, God himself did. The children of Israel had to learn to trust only in the Lord, for only He could be their salvation. If they trusted in me for miracles, they would have learned nothing—and the world could never be blessed because of our nation."

"But what wrong did you do?" you plead.

"I will tell you. During all the years of bondage

in Egypt, and all the years in the desert, Israel was learning that to be God's people, they needed only to trust in Him. They were a stiff-necked people, and did not learn this quickly.

When God displayed His mighty power in delivering us from the hands of Pharaoh, the people began to learn to trust Him. He displayed His power and His love for His people over and over again during our years in the wilderness, and then, just when the lesson was almost learned, I did something that took their trust away from the Lord, and directed it at myself." Moses' voice falters, and his face is sad.

You continue to watch him, mystified.

After a pause, Moses continues. "In the Desert of Zin, there was no water for the congregation; they grumbled and complained, much as usual. The Lord told Aaron and me that we should take the rod and speak to the rock before the assembly. The rock would then yield water, and the people and animals could drink. But I did not do as the Lord had commanded me. I struck the rock with the rod, and said to the people, 'Listen now, you rebels; shall we bring forth water for you from this rock?'" Moses' voice fades into silence.

"But what was so wrong with that?" you ask.

"Because the people might have believed that *I* brought the water gushing from the rock, and not the Lord. Even Egyptian priests can do magic tricks," says Moses strongly.

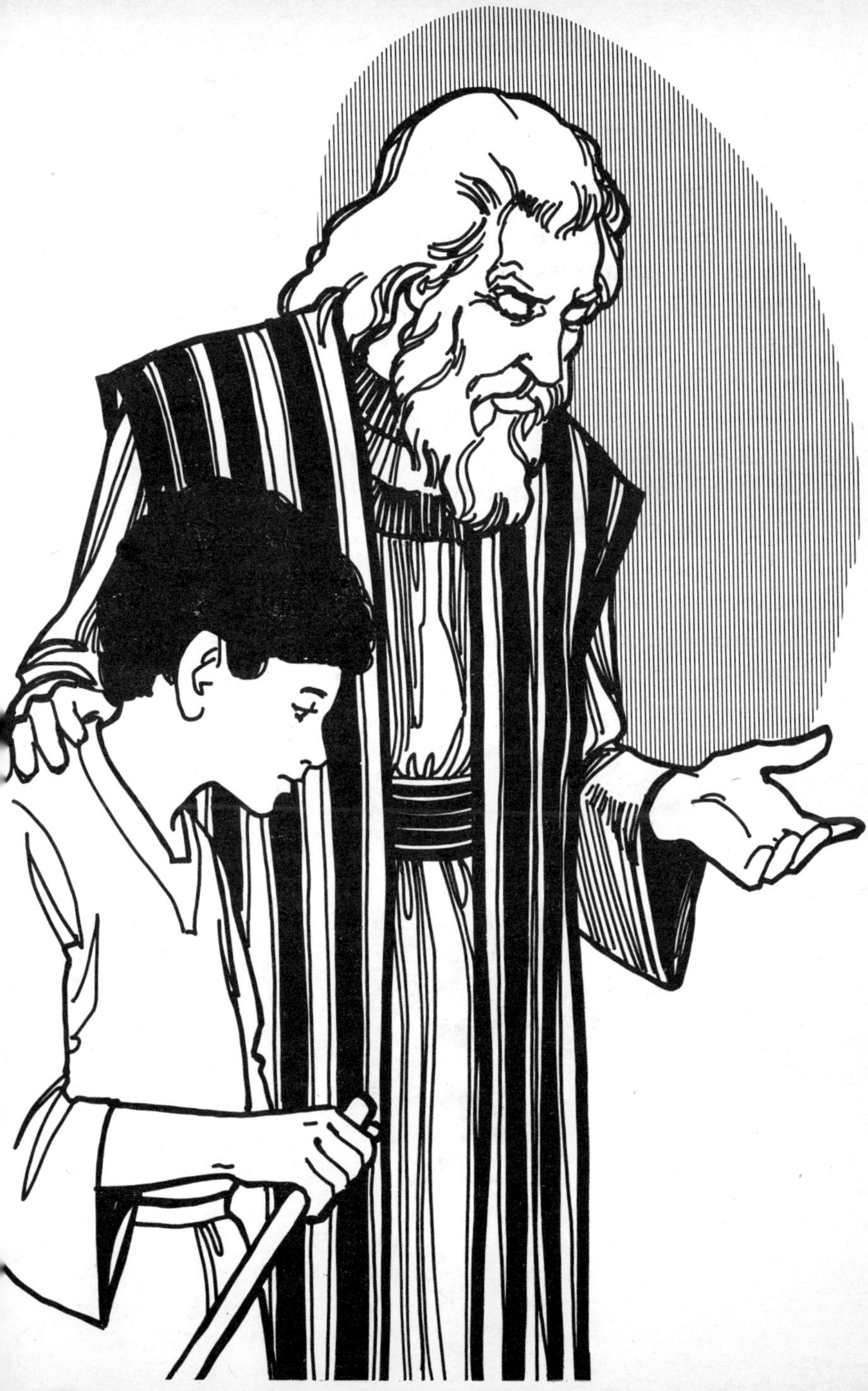

You gasp as you realize the enormity of Moses' sin.

"And now, my son, I must go on up the mountain. I will proclaim the name of the Lord. Oh, praise the greatness of our God! He is the Rock, His works are perfect, and all His ways are just. A faithful God who does no wrong, upright and just is He."

Moses begins the climb up Mount Nebo, but turns and smiles once more at you. You feel humbled and grateful, and wave with love at this mighty man of God.

Reluctantly, you turn away, and find your chariot waiting silently. You realize that your quest is finished. You climb aboard the chariot to return home, realizing that you can never be quite the same person again.

THE END

(You Have Decided to Stay With Joshua)

All the people around you are watching Moses make his way slowly across the plain. Silent tears are streaming down many faces, and others sob openly.

"There will never again be a prophet like Moses," the man standing next to you says quietly. "The Lord knew Moses face-to-face. Through him, God showed His mighty power and performed awesome deeds in the sight of all Israel."

Voices around you murmur agreement. You think about asking these people why Moses is not allowed to cross the Jordan, but they are grief stricken, and you find that you do not want to add to their pain.

You glance at Joshua, and see that he too is overcome with grief. You remember that he has been close to Moses for years, so he must feel like he has just lost a father. You decide that you will have to try to follow Moses.

You walk swiftly through the mourning people, breaking into a run as you find yourself in the open plain. Ahead of you is Mount Nebo, and you can just see the solitary figure of Moses making his way toward the mountain. You run as fast as you can, taking great gulps of air into your dry, aching lungs. At last, you arrive at the foot of Mount Nebo and stop, panting. Moses has just begun his ascent of the mountain.

Go to page 100.

(You Have Gone Forward in Time, in Midian)

Scarcely before you are aware of leaving, you find yourself alone again. The tents are behind you, and you hear the familiar sounds of the Midianites stirring in the early morning. In the timeless sweep of life in the desert, nothing has changed.

"Father! May I go with you this morning?" you hear a young voice cry. You turn, and see a young boy running eagerly to greet his father; you realize that the boy's father is Moses.

"Not this morning, son. I must speak with your grandfather about something very important," says Moses slowly.

Disappointed, the boy nods. He watches his father go inside his grandfather's tent, then kneels quietly by the side of the tent. *It's a lot easier to eavesdrop with tents than with houses*, you think to yourself. You decide to listen, too.

Kneeling on the ground by the tent, you hear Moses and Jethro talking earnestly.

"Let me go back to my own people in Egypt, to see if any of them are still alive," Moses implores.

"Go, then," says Jethro kindly, "and I wish you well."

Hastily, you scramble up from your position by the tent; you notice that Moses's son looks frightened and unsure. The day passes quickly, as Moses and his wife and sons make preparations

Decide Your Own Adventure

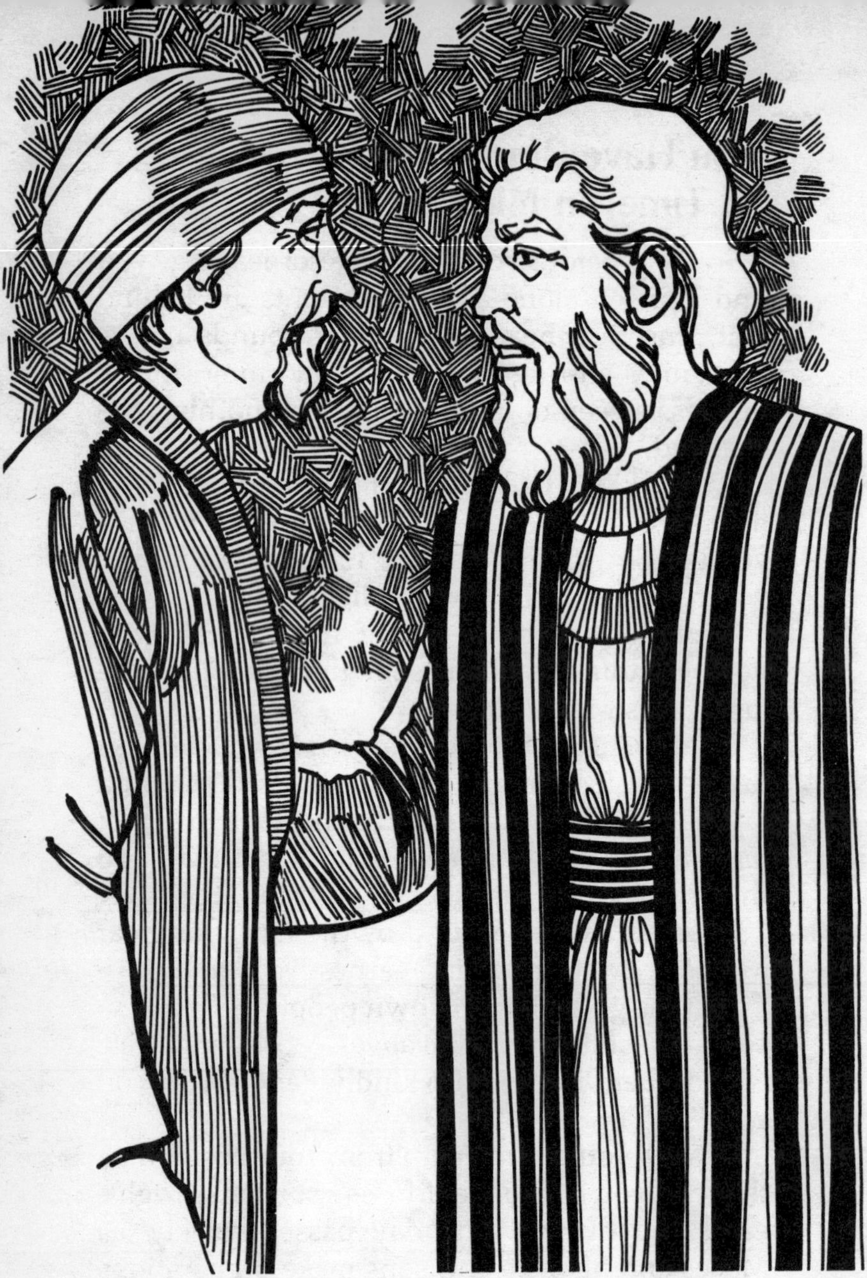

to leave the next morning. Everyone is whispering about Moses.

You find that you are still accepted as belonging here as readily as you were forty years before. You see a young man helping Moses with his preparations, and when he is finished, you ask curiously, "Why is Moses leaving Midian, do you know?"

"Certainly," he answers slowly, "but I'm not sure that it makes any sense. Moses says that He-Who-Has-No-Name spoke to him face-to-face in the desert yesterday. He says that He appeared in a bush that was alive with flames, yet was not consumed by fire. And Moses says that he must return to Egypt to see if any of his own people are still alive. It seems awfully foolish to me, but Jethro loves him dearly, and will allow Moses to do whatever he wishes.

"So they are to leave tomorrow?" you ask.

"Yes, at first light," the young man answers.

You watch Moses the remainder of the day—he looks frightened, yet resolute. You wonder if you'll be allowed to go with him, or if you'll have to stay here. You wonder if you would have the courage or the faith to walk into a situation as full of danger as this situation that Moses faces.

Evening falls, and you wander out a little way into the desert to watch for the stars to twinkle into life. Somehow, you are not surprised to see that the chariot awaits you just over the crest of a small rise of land.

The voice carries clear as crystal in the night air. "You will go forward in time again. You may choose to join Moses at some point in the future, or to join the family of Semnet and Hapu again. Do not be alarmed—they will not wonder at your being the same age; you will be accepted there, as here. What is your choice?"

You admire Moses greatly, and want very much to stay with him; but you'd also like to see Semnet and Hapu again. You remember that you still have things to learn on your quest, and are unsure which decision would be the best. You take the reins into your hands as you mount, debating between your choices.

If you decide to join the family of Semnet, go to page 93.

If you decide to stay with Moses, go to page 89.

(You Have Come to a Time Near the End of the Journey)

You find yourself on a hill overlooking the Israeli encampment. Tents are pitched across the plain, covering the low hills that loom in the west. You notice that there seem to be only a few more tents than there were almost forty years ago. You decide that even though none of the 600,000 grumblers who left Egypt would be allowed to cross over into Canaan, they all had descendants who would.

From your vantage point on the hill, you can see most of the tents. As far as you can tell, all the people have left their tents and are moving toward the center of the camp. *They must be on their way to the tent of meeting*, you think, for you know that is in the center. You decide to join the mass of moving people.

Soon, you are walking through a crowd of people, all surging forward to the tabernacle. Excitement is in their voices, for they are at last within sight of their promised land. The call from the silver trumpets has summoned them to assemble, and they are eager to hear what their beloved Moses has to tell them.

A friendly-looking young man falls into step beside you, and says, "Is it not wonderful how the mighty hand of the Lord gives us victory over all our enemies? If the Lord is with us, who can stand against us?"

You agree heartily, and he continues. "Have you seen the land that we will enter tomorrow? It is a good land that we go to!" He breaks into a delighted laugh, and claps you on the back in friendship.

You notice that in this crowd you hear no grumbling, but only praise for the Lord—it is a happy, rejoicing group, and you are glad to be here. But strangely, you feel an undercurrent of sadness; you wonder why. The crowd about you comes to a stop. You stand on tiptoe, and see Moses waiting to speak to the throng.

The Moses you see before you is very old—one hundred and twenty years, you remember. His hair is silver, and his face is worn with care. But his eyes have remained the same, and his voice is still forceful and strong. He raises his hand in blessing over the people he has led for so long, and speaks.

"Hear now, O Israel, what I am about to say." The assembly falls silent, intent on every word.

"I shall not cross the Jordan with you; Joshua will be your new leader." The people grow even more still.

"Ask now about the former days long before your time, from the day God created man on the earth; ask from one end of the heavens to the other. Has anything so great as this ever happened, or has anything like it ever been heard of? Has any other people heard the voice of God speaking out of fire, as you have, and lived? Has

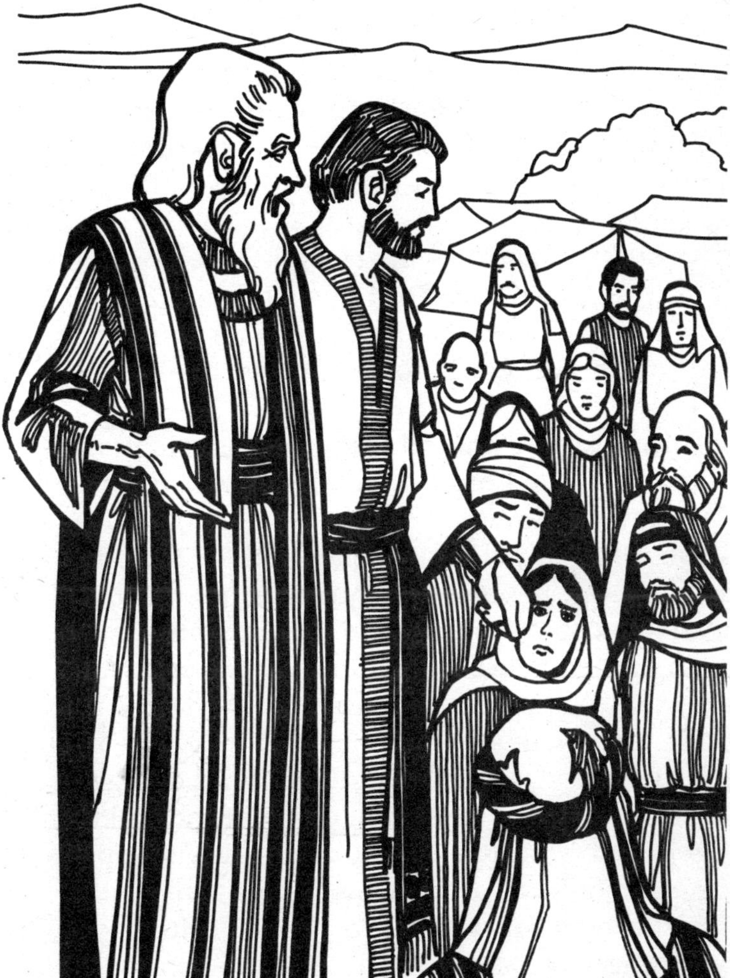

any god ever tried to take for himself one nation out of another nation, by testings, by miraculous signs and wonders, by war, by a mighty hand and an outstretched arm, or by great and awesome deeds, like all the things the Lord your God did for you in Egypt before your very eyes?"

Moses smiles lovingly at his people before him. "You were shown these things so that you might know that the Lord is God; besides Him there is no other."

Moses' voice grows in strength and vibrance, "Hear, O Israel: The Lord our God, the Lord is one! Love the Lord your God with all your heart and with all your soul and with all your strength."

Voices from all around you join Moses in praise and love, "The Lord our God, the Lord is one!"

Moses continues, "Fear the Lord your God, serve Him only. Do not follow other gods, the gods of the peoples around you; for the Lord your God is a jealous God and his anger will burn against you. In the future, when your sons ask you, 'What is the meaning of these laws?' tell them, 'We were slaves of Pharaoh in Egypt, but the Lord brought us out of Egypt with a mighty hand. Before our eyes the Lord sent miraculous signs and wonders—great and terrible—upon Egypt and Pharaoh and his whole household.' Your forefathers who went down into Egypt were the twelve sons of Jacob and their families—seventy in all—and now the Lord has made

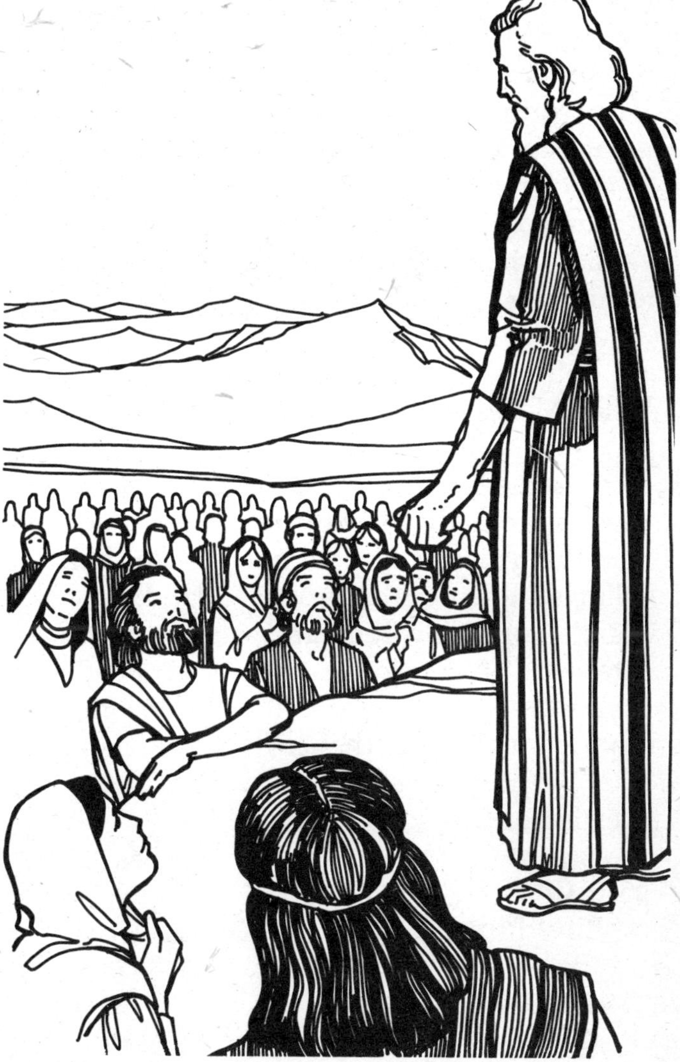

you as numerous as the stars in the sky."

Like a flash of lightening, you realize that these Hebrews are now a *people:* one in spirit and purpose, forged into one through faith amid trials. They speak as one in praise of God, who took a down-trodden collection of humanity from bondage and selfish concerns, to faith in himself, the only One who can make us truly free.

Moses continues to speak, and you feel the love these children of Israel bear him. "Be strong and courageous. Do not be afraid or terrified, for the Lord your God goes with you; He will never leave you nor forsake you."

When Moses is finished speaking, the crowd is silent. Joshua is the leader now, and will lead them into the land that God has promised them. Moses slips quietly away through the crowd. You realize that you still do not know why he will not be allowed to enter the promised land.

Should you follow him, and ask him to explain the reason? You are hesitant to be so bold, and yet you are certain he would understand. Or should you stay in the crowd and listen to Joshua, in the hope that he will explain why Moses is not going into Canaan?

**If you decide
to follow Moses, go to page 36.**

**If you decide
to stay with Joshua, go to page 105.**

(You Have Decided to Go to School)

"I guess I'll try the school," you say weakly, thinking with dismay about how good your school sounds compared with schools where the teachers are allowed to beat the students.

The Egyptian beams his approval and thumps you on the back heartily. "Good choice, son—we're almost there. Then you may come on home with my son afterward."

You begin to take more notice of your surroundings, and see that as you have been walking, you have reached the city limits—you are now walking briskly along a dusty street, lined on both sides with houses made from sun-baked bricks, whitewashed and sparkling. The road bends to the right, and as you round the bend, you are amazed at what you see.

Far down the road rises a massive structure of red stone, seeming to stretch for as far as you can see. Huge pylons frame the entrance, and crowds of people are everywhere. Here, the street is paved with black stone, and almost everywhere you look, statues line the road. Not noticing your amazement, the Egyptian hurries you along to a small doorway in the huge red building, well away from the pylons that frame the entrance.

He bustles you inside, where your jaw drops in surprise. You find yourself in an open terrace, lined with enormous, hieroglyphic-covered columns. Beyond the cool, shaded terrace you see beautiful, sunlit gardens--tall palm trees sway gently, and the delicate smell of jasmine floats gently in the breeze. You'd like to just stop walking, to stop right here and enjoy looking around, but the Egyptian hurries you across a corner of the garden, and into a small stone building.

Oh, oh—this must be the school, you think, as your stomach develops a terrible sinking feeling. About twenty boys, all ages from about five years on up, sit cross-legged on the cool, stone floor. They are all wearing a simple linen garment like yours, and not one of them looks up at the interruption. They are bent over wooden boards resting on their knees, and they are using

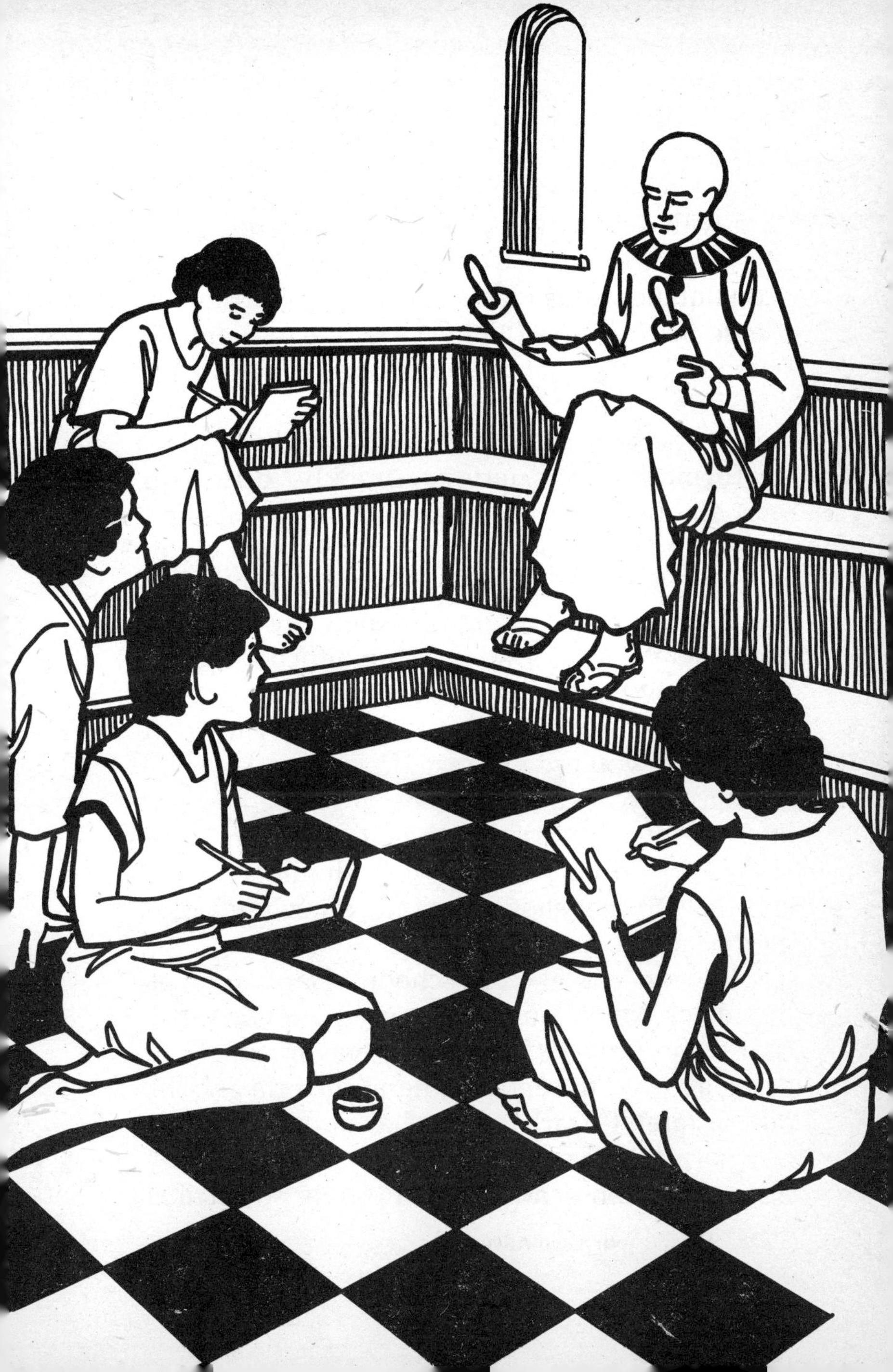

brushes that they dip into a small bowl just in front of them.

The Egyptian man is talking to a stern-looking man with a shaved head and no-nonsense eyes. They seem to come to an agreement, and your acquaintance nods reassuringly as he hurries out the door. The rest of the very long day seems to pass in a blur—you have never worked so hard at school in your life!

The priest—for that is who the bald man is—performed introductions quickly, and you learned that "your" Egyptian's son is named Hapu, and that you are expected to copy hieroglyphics nonstop, from sunrise to sunset. Surprisingly, you found that you knew the meaning of the symbols, so it was not too difficult to copy them—only tedious. No one looked up from his work unless the priest directed it; and by the end of the day, you are exhausted.

At last the priest smiles—he might be human, after all—and dismisses you all for the day. Hapu claps a friendly arm about your shoulders, and, shortly, you are relieved to find yourself in a cool garden, just before the sun sets.

"How did you like our school?" Hapu asks, as he rushes you through the garden, and onto the cool stone terrace. "My father was fortunate in being allowed to send me there; the other scribe schools aren't nearly as good as ours!" You realize that you have absolutely no wish to see any other Egyptian school if this one is so terrific!

Together you hurry along the terrace, and out again onto the street. You cast a quick look over your shoulder at the massive building, glowing warmly red in the light of the setting sun.

"We're home," Hapu shouts happily, as he stops in front of a two-story home of whitewashed brick. He pauses expectantly, his hand on the door, waiting for you to follow him.

You realize that your quest seems farther and farther away. How are you ever going to discover why God would not allow Moses to enter the promised land, if you're stuck in Egypt when Moses is a baby? On the other hand, in Hapu's home you might learn something useful—and you badly need some food and rest. Should you stay, or should you run away and try to find out if the chariot of fire appears when you need it? You have to decide, because Hapu is looking very puzzled as you stand, undecided, outside his house.

If you decide to go inside Hapu's house, turn to page 65.

If you decide to run away to find the chariot, turn to page 52.

(You Have Decided to See the Tabernacle)

You find yourself in the hot, shimmering desert—within sight of the vast camp of Hebrews. In addition to the normal sounds of the bleating of goats, children playing, and women preparing meals, you hear the sound of busy hammering and the unmistakable sounds of many people working.

You walk toward the camp, noticing that there seems to be groups of tents. Each group has its own banner, and you wonder if this is the beginning of the twelve tribes of Israel. There are so many people that it takes you a long time to make your way through the tents to the center of the vast encampment. As you wind your way through the maze of tents, you notice that everyone is working busily.

You see one boy who isn't working; he is aimlessly scratching in the dust with a stick.

"What's going on?" you ask him.

"Where have you been?" he says, staring at you curiously. "For three months now, everyone has been helping to build the tabernacle. My father says that tomorrow it will be set up, since tomorrow is the first day of the first month." His brow furrows as he continues. "I wanted to go inside when they get it set up, but Moses says that only Aaron and his sons are allowed to go in, because they're the priests. I wish I could be a priest," he finishes mournfully.

"Is *everyone* working on the tabernacle?" you ask in amazement. "I thought it was just a tent!"

"Just a tent!" the boy hoots scornfully. "Here, come with me. I'll show you some of the things they're making to go inside the 'tent'!"

You follow the boy, who says his name is Eleazar. As you walk, he shows you men sweating over a fire, forging something from silver. Further on, you watch craftsmen carefully overlaying huge wooden posts with gold. Still others are busy finishing golden hooks. The work you see is obviously last-minute touches on a huge project that is almost completed.

Men and women hurry to and fro, carrying beautifully-woven cloths, and brilliantly-died skins. You catch glimpses of gold, silver, and bronze everywhere—as well as the flash of polished gems. Eleazar smiles at your astonishment. "Now do you think that it's 'just a tent'?" he laughs.

You and Eleazar spend the remainder of the day trying to stay out of the way in the cheerful bustle of workers putting the finishing touches on their contributions. Excitement hums in the air, for everyone is looking forward to the next day, when all will be ready, and the tabernacle will be set up. You find that you are excited too. Eleazar takes you back to his tent, where you are welcomed. You are glad to lie down on a mat, but sleep does not come quickly on this night.

You wake with a feeling of anticipation—this is the day! Eleazar's family is stirring already, buzzing with excitement, although it is not yet dawn. You are itching to go and watch the tabernacle being set up, but Eleazar's father tells you with a smile that none of you will go until Moses tells you it is time. Disappointed, you and Eleazar wait silently.

At last, the time arrives. All the Hebrews are pouring out of their tents, thronging to the tent of meeting—the tabernacle. You slip eagerly through the crowd, arriving at a good vantage point from which to view the newly-erected wonder. You gasp in amazement at what you see before you.

At the entrance to the tent of meeting stands Moses, with his brother Aaron and Aaron's sons. The crowd is hushed and expectant.

"This is what the Lord has commanded to be done," says Moses, as he carefully washes Aaron and his sons with water. Moses then places a tunic upon Aaron, ties a sash around him, and clothes him with a beautiful blue robe that has intricately-embroidered pomegranates and bells of pure gold around the hem. Next, he carefully adds two more garments—you are uncertain what they are—and places a turban on Aaron's head. The ordination of Aaron and his sons continues, but people crowd in front of you and you are unable to see any more.

Decide Your Own Adventure 125

You crane your neck to look at the tabernacle, for it is beautiful and awesome. You can hear Moses beginning to speak again, and you strain to hear.

"What has been done today was commanded by the Lord to make atonement for you." Then turning to Aaron, Moses continues "The process of ordaining you and your sons to the priesthood will continue for seven days. You must stay at the entrance to the tent of meeting day and night for seven days, and do what the Lord requires. And for generations to come, these sacred garments will belong to your descendants."

The assembly of people slowly disperses, with many casting backwards glances at the beautiful tabernacle.

The next seven days pass swiftly with Eleazar and his family. At the end of seven days, you are all called back to the tent of meeting.

This time, it is impossible for you to get close enough to see or hear anything that is going on. For a long time you stand, wondering what is going on. But, as Aaron begins his duties as priest, a hush falls over the crowd, and you can hear Aaron blessing the people. You stand on tiptoe, and see Moses and Aaron going into the tent of meeting. When they come out, they bless everyone again.

An expectant hush falls over the assembled people. You see that everyone is looking up, so you follow their gaze. Coming to rest over the

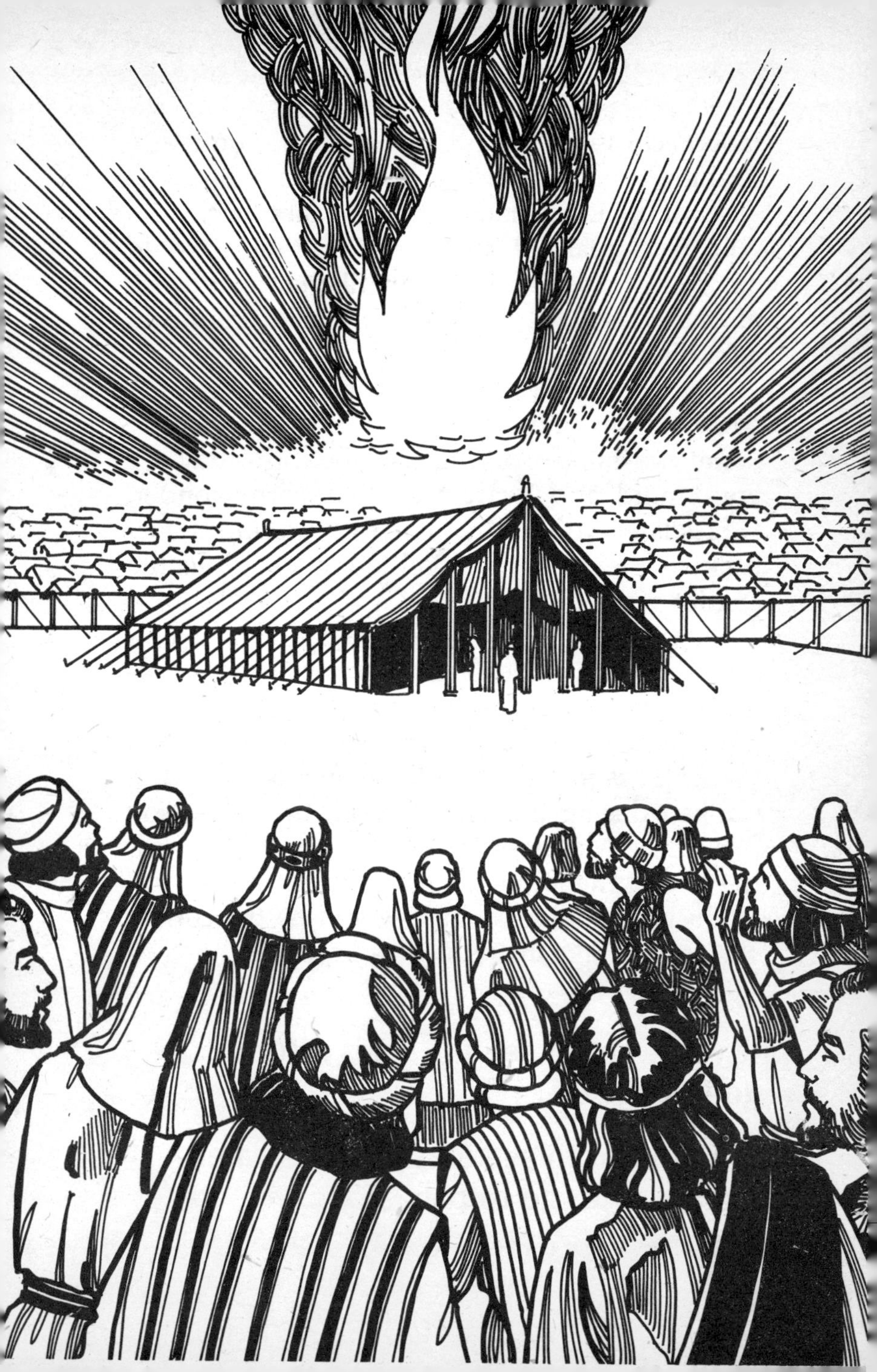

tabernacle is an enormous pillar of cloud, fire flashing from its midst. You have read about the glory of the Lord that covered the tabernacle, but you never realized how awe-inspiring it would be. Shouts of joy and worship fill the air, and as if of one accord, all present fall to the ground in adoration.

"The Lord now dwells among us," you hear someone murmur quietly.

You remember nothing else about this day, for your mind and heart are filled with wonder. Hours later, you find yourself wandering slowly back to Eleazar's tent. Behind it, you see the chariot waiting.

"It is time to travel again," says the voice quietly. "You may choose between two events during the journey of the children of Israel. You will find yourself in Kadesh-barnea for either. Will you witness the return of the men who spied out Canaan during the second year, or would you like to see Moses bring water from a rock near the end of the jouney? The choice is up to you."

You have no idea which would be the correct choice. You take the reins in your hands thoughtfully.

If you want to see the spies return, go to page 84.

If you want to see Moses bring water from a rock, go to page 75.

(You Have Decided to Go Forward in Time)

You are glad that you have decided to go forward in time, as you find yourself in the desert. Your arrival is unnoticed in the outer fringes of a huge crowd of people. You see multitudes of tents pitched in the distance, so you know that for now, at least, the Hebrews are not traveling. You wonder how much time has elapsed since the crossing of the Red Sea.

"Isn't this a wonderful life that Moses has led us to?" a voice near you whines. The crowd grumbles general agreement, and you look around you in surprise.

"Only forty-five days ago, we were in Egypt—and now we enjoy the wonderful attraction of the Desert of Sin!" an angry-sounding woman says, looking around at others for their approval.

"If only we had died by the Lord's hand in Egypt! There we sat around pots of meat and ate all the food we wanted, but Moses has brought us into this desert to starve the entire assembly to death!"

You are surprised that these people—and there are many—have so quickly forgotten the passover, and the crossing of the Red Sea. How can they dare grumble? You decide that you'd rather not be with this crowd, and make your way toward the encampment of tents, hoping to find Moses.

As you walk through the tents, you hear the same angry muttering and whispering coming from everyone. All seem to be angry at Moses, and sorry they ever left the "joys of captivity" in Egypt. It seems as if the entire huge throng of people has forgotten what the mighty hand of the Lord has done for them.

You see the easily-recognizable figure of Moses nearby, and arrive at his side just in time to hear him talking urgently with Aaron, his brother.

"Summon the entire Israelite community. Tell them, 'Come before the Lord, for he has heard your grumbling.'"

Moses looks troubled and worn as Aaron hurries away, and you decide that this is not a very good time to talk to him. You stay close to his tent, and watch the Hebrews begin to congregate, looking resentful and surly.

In a short while, the multitude is waiting, and Moses begins to speak.

"In the evening, you will know that it was the Lord who brought you out of Egypt, and in the morning you will see the glory of the Lord, because he has heard your grumbling against Him."

Some of the people nearest you begin to look uneasy, and Moses continues.

"You will know that it was the Lord when He gives you meat to eat in the evening and all the bread you want in the morning, because He has heard your grumbling against Him. Who are we?

You are not grumbling against us, but against the Lord!"

Now quite a few people look guilty and troubled, and as Moses wheels around and disappears inside his tent, nearly everyone rushes away, their eyes lowered uncomfortably. It is nearly dusk, and you feel weary. You stretch out in the shade of Moses' tent, and fall into a light sleep.

You are startled by the sound of excited voices. Raising yourself to one elbow, you glance in the direction of the noise. You are amazed to see huge flocks of quail cover the entire camp, as far as the eye can see. People are delightedly catching the birds, knowing that they will eat well tonight, without having to expend much effort at all. You see Moses standing silently in the flap of his tent, watching.

He beckons you into his tent with a smile, and you go gladly. Although you are afraid to speak to such a mighty man of God, it is comforting to be near him. He seems not to mind your silence, and he and Aaron share their dinner with you. You listen to their conversation, and fall easily to sleep as the night deepens.

You wake refreshed. Dawn colors the sky, and the air smells unusually pleasant. Moses and Aaron are gone. Yawning, you stretch mightily and stroll outside the tent. Yet another amazing sight greets you.

The early morning dew on the ground is

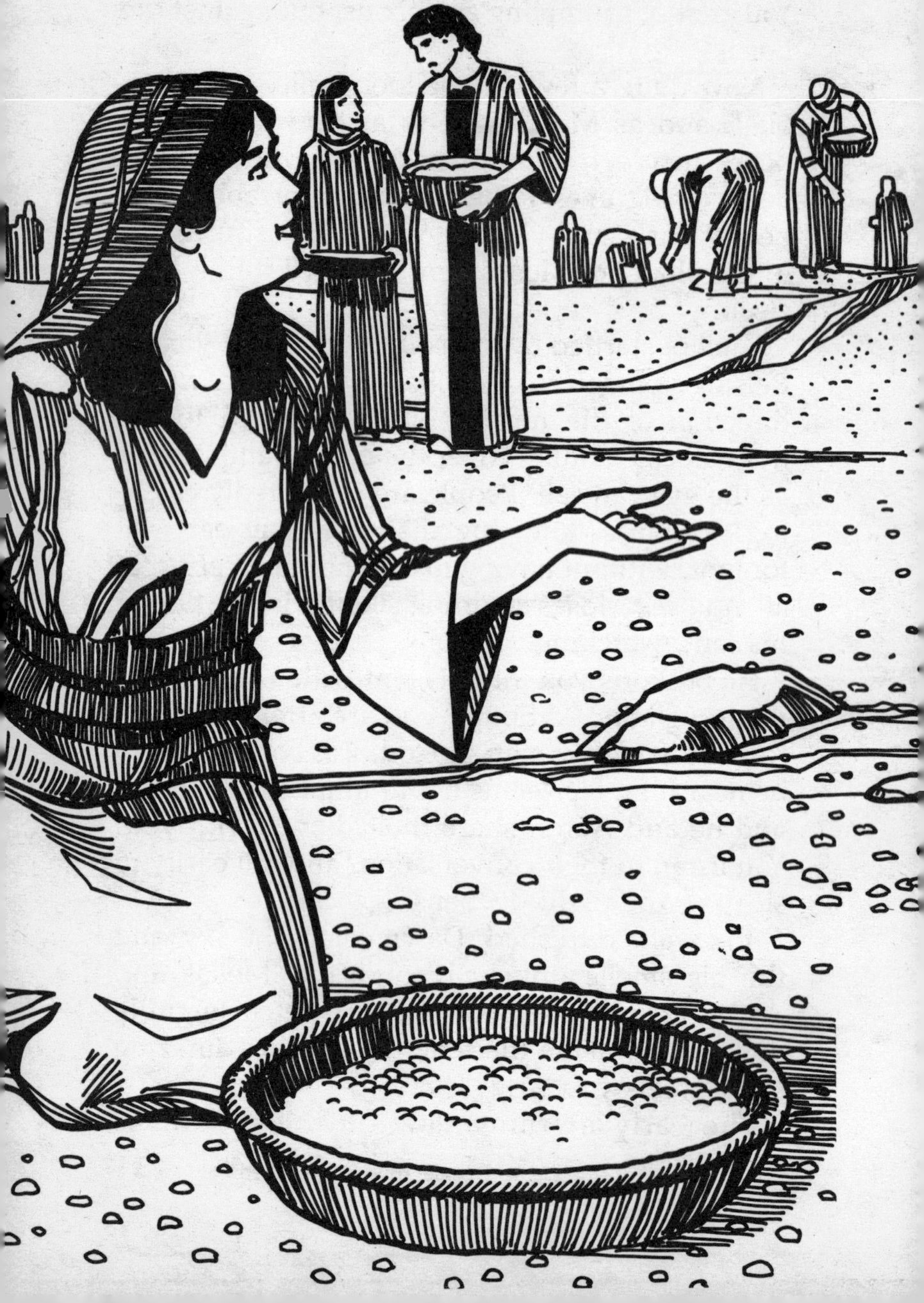

gone—and in its place is a fine, flake-like substance, looking almost like frost.

"What is it?" you hear many voices murmur, as they stare in puzzlement at the ground.

Moses calls out in a voice loud and strong, "It is the bread which the Lord has given you to eat."

You listen while he explains how much of it they are to gather. More and more sleepy Hebrews come from their tents, rubbing their eyes at the sight that greets them. You pick up a bit, and look at Moses questioningly. He nods, and you taste it. To your surprise, it is light and sweet. *After eating this, how could anyone want anything else?* you wonder.

You can begin to feel the arrival of the chariot, so you walk quietly around behind the tent. Sure enough, it awaits you.

So far, you have seen Moses do nothing for which he should be ashamed. You thoughtfully mount the chariot, wondering what your choices will be this time.

"You may go forward to the time of the giving of the law at Mount Sinai, or farther forward to near the end of the journeying of the children of Israel. Which would you prefer?" says the voice.

You wonder if Moses did something to displease God when he was receiving the law. Or, perhaps he became discouraged near the end of his journey and that's when he made his mistake. You take the reins into your hands.

If you decide to go to the time when Moses receives the law, turn to page 45.

If you decide to go to the time near the end of the journey, turn to page 111.

(You Have Decided to See the Crossing of the Red Sea)

You find yourself at the edge of a vast number of people; you have never been in such a huge group. You remember that there were supposed to be about *six hundred thousand* men on foot, besides women and children. *There must be almost two million people here,* you think with awe. You wonder how Moses is ever going to control this large a number.

The ground you are standing on is slightly elevated so you can see far ahead to the sea. On another rise at the edge of the sea, you see a lone figure standing—you wonder if it might be Moses. Also at the edge of the sea, in front of this huge crowd, is the strangest cloud you have ever seen; it looks like a tornado except it is still!

You skirt the edge of the throng of people, making your way as quickly as you can toward the solitary figure standing on the low hill. Your plan is to get close to Moses and to find out what the strange cloud means. As you walk, you hear a frightened murmur spreading like a wave among the people.

"The Egyptians are coming! Look over there!"

You look in the direction of many pointing arms, and see clouds of dust low on the distant horizon. It is difficult to tell, but the dust clouds are probably many miles away. You quicken your steps, and soon reach the hill; it is indeed Moses standing there. The frightened murmur has swelled to a frenzy, and the words, "The Egyptians are coming! They will murder us all!" finally reach Moses.

"Was it because there were no graves in Egypt that you brought us to the desert to die?" wails a man standing right beside you. Moses turns to look at him. "What have you done to us by bringing us out of Egypt?"

Yet another voice takes up the complaint, "Didn't we say to you in Egypt, 'Leave us alone; let us serve the Egyptians'? It would have been better for us to serve the Egyptians than to die here in the desert!"

Your jaw drops in amazement; how can they so soon forget the power they experienced during the plagues and on the night of passover?

Moses looks unperturbed, and he faces the

terrified people calmly. "Do not be afraid. Stand firm and you will see the deliverance the Lord will bring you today. The Egyptians you see today you will never see again. The Lord will fight for you; you need only to be still."

These words seem to have a calming effect on those around you. Moses' words are passed along to those out of the immediate hearing range, and slowly, quietness spreads in all directions. You shift your position, looking between shoulders at the horizon beyond Moses. It is then that you see the immense pillar of cloud begin to move, and your scalp prickles. The pillar seems to stretch from the ground straight up into Heaven! Others have begun to notice the movement too, and excited shouts spread through the multitude.

"Look!" someone near you shouts, "The pillar that has been guiding us is now going behind us!"

"Oh, what can that mean?" someone else wails. "Are we to turn around and march straight into the weapons of Pharaoh's men?"

At last, the pillar ceases to move—it is between the children of Israel and the approaching Egyptians, hiding one group from the other. And, although evening had been turning into night, brilliant light from the cloud now pours over all the Hebrews. Yet, from your vantage point on

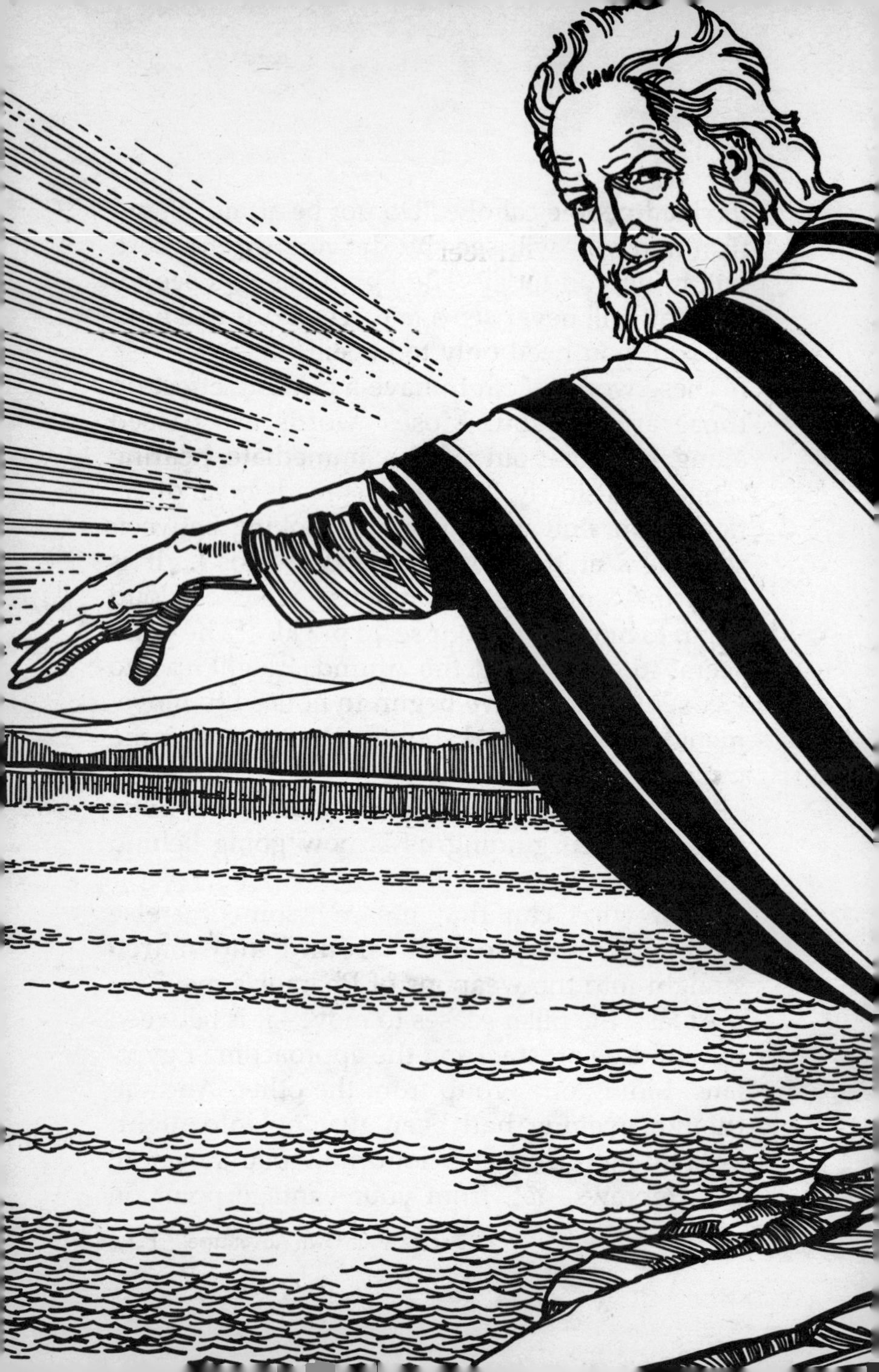

the hill, you can see that behind the great pillar of cloud, all the land lies in darkness. You shiver at this awesome display of God's power over day and night. You can feel that the peoples' dread has ebbed, and all around you, you hear sighs of relief.

You glance at Moses, and see that he has stretched out his hand over the sea, and at his command, a strong east wind has begun to rise. Fiercer and fiercer the wind blows, whipping the water on the sea into a white-foamed frenzy. Wave piles upon wave, in an ever-growing tower of seething turbulence. Power throbs in the very air you breathe, until you are almost forced to your knees by the sheer weight of it.

The people around you are silent, and they look with awestricken faces at the sea before them. All night long the fierce wind will blow, driving and holding the water back, while drying a path that stretches all the way to the other side of the Red Sea. At a command from Moses the entire company begins to move steadily between the towering walls of sea on either side. Men, women, children, animals—all move silently between the walls of the miracle. On their faces is a mixture of fear and awe. Fear of entering the seabed between the massive walls of shimmering water, fear of Pharaoh's army that is still behind them, and awesome fear of the great God almighty who has heard their grumbles and lack of faith.

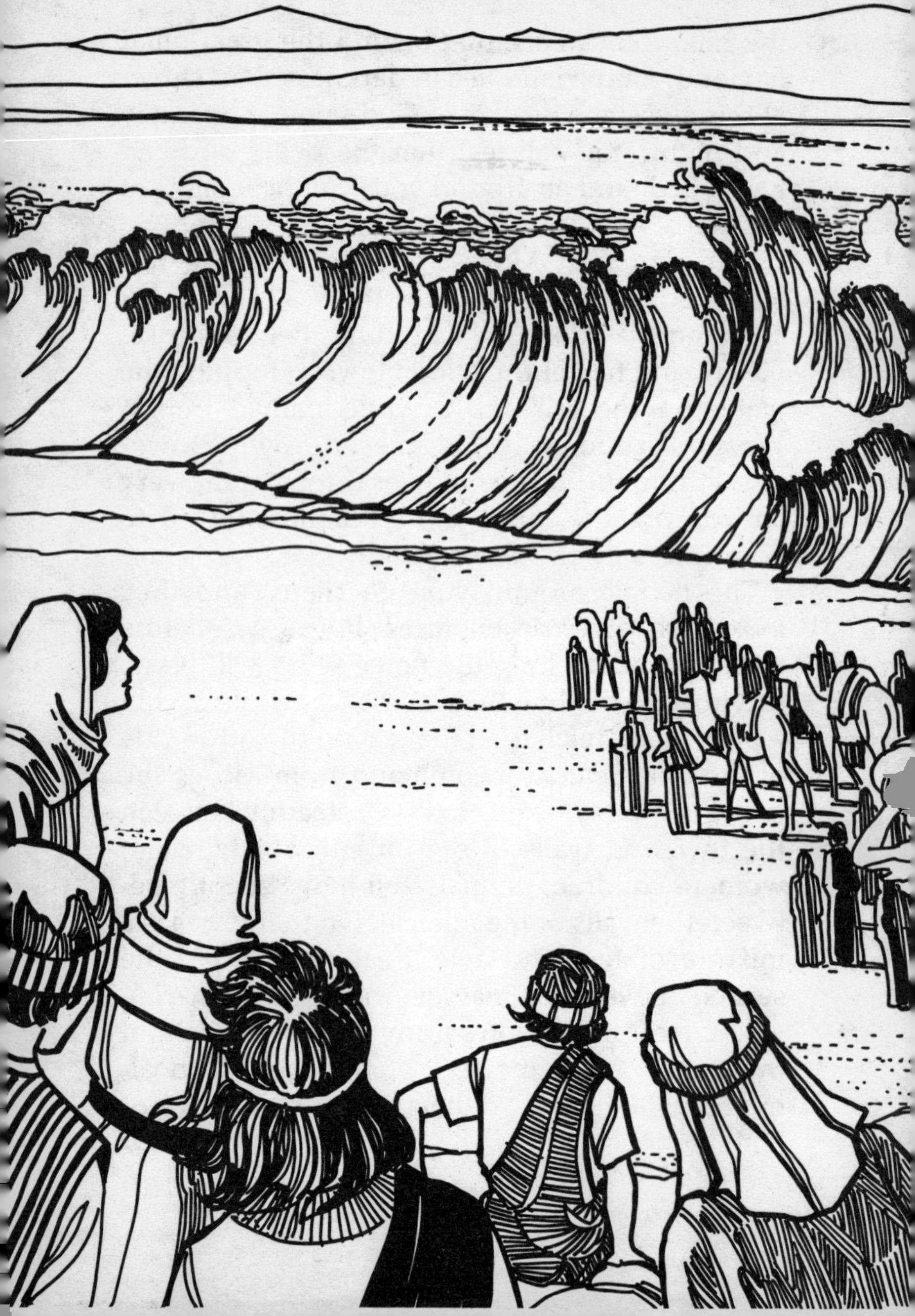

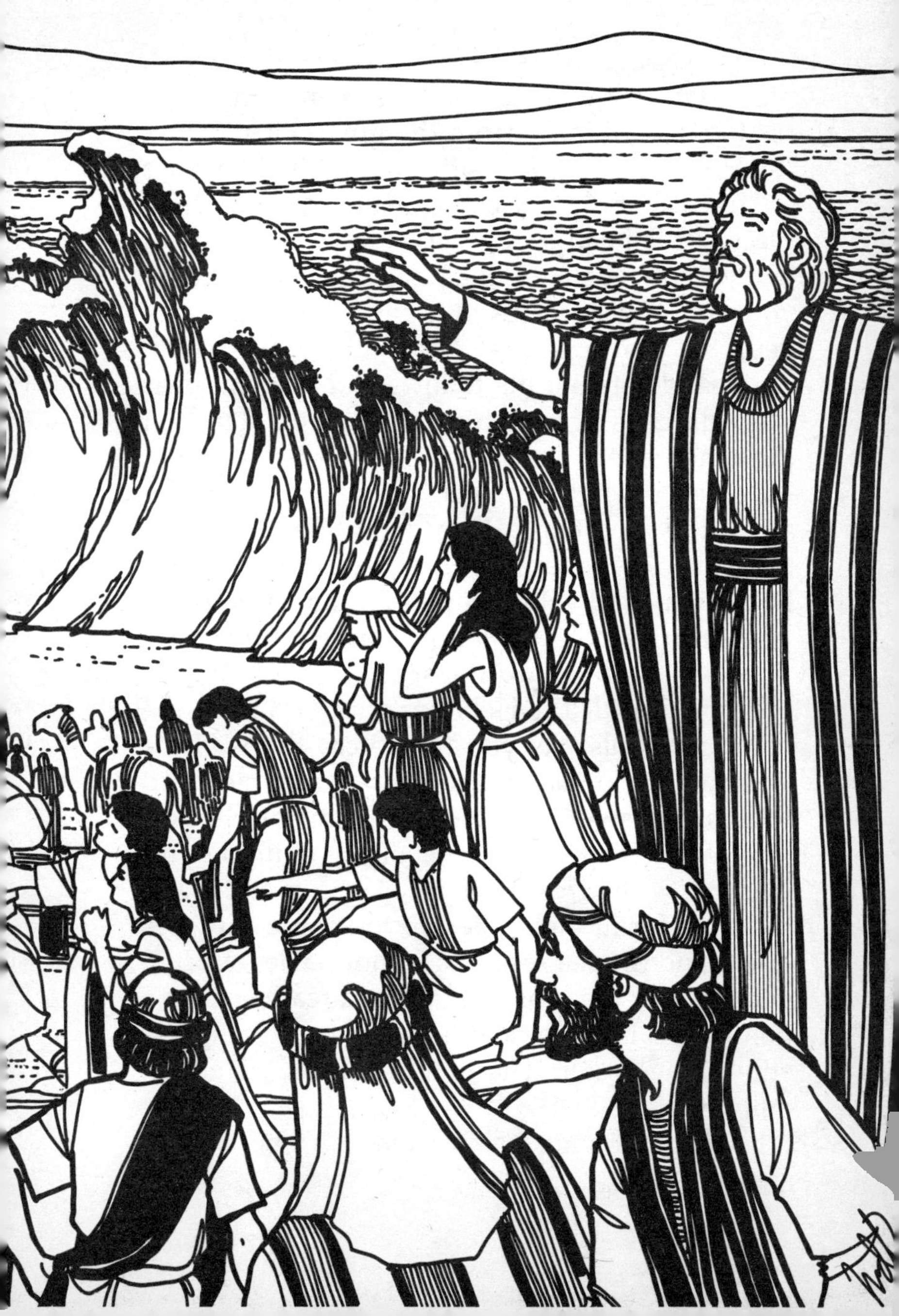

The passage across the dry sea bed takes all night—at least what *would* have been night if not for the light shining from the great pillar. When the Hebrew multitude is finally on the other side of the sea, the great cloud resumes its original place at the head of the mass of Hebrew people, and you can again see the Egyptian army hard on your trail. Their horses thunder onto the dry seabed, the warriors they bear thirsty for battle. Thousands of chariots follow, and you can hear the wild cries of rage from where you stand on the other side.

But as daylight breaks, confusion seems to strike the Egyptians. They wheel about crazily, their chariots swerving in every direction. You hear frightened yells from their number now. As you turn to look at Moses, you see him again raise his hand toward the sea.

"Look! Look!" the Hebrews cry, pointing to the huge sea walls. As you all watch, the walls of water begin to collapse, crashing over men and horses, and sweeping the entire army off the bottom of the seabed. Screams of the dying Egyptians mix with screams of the Hebrews at the awful, wonderful sight. Before long, the din dies down and the sea resumes its normal level. Here and there, a piece of clothing or a feather from a helmet can be seen floating on the surface of the still-rolling water. The children of Israel are finally free.

In the following celebration, no one notices

you slip quietly away from the group, for your chariot awaits you at a little distance. You are still awed at all you have seen, and climb quietly into the chariot. As before, the voice is clear. "You may choose to go forward in time, or backward. It would probably be best if you chose forward."

You remember that you still have not found out why Moses will not be allowed to enter the promised land. Could the answer lie back in time, or should you follow the suggested course? You grasp the reins firmly and make your decision.

If you decide to go back in time, go to page 20.

If you decide to go forward in time, go to page 129.

(You Want to Try the Shortcut)

Somehow, your steed seems to know your decision without your having to speak. You pull the smooth leather of the reins taut, and suddenly...

Go to page 11.

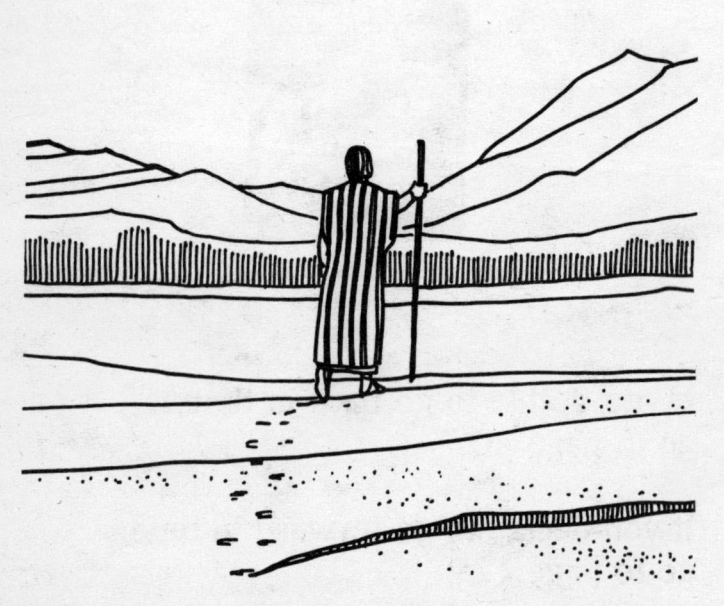